The Magic Chip

EXPLORING MICROELECTRONICS

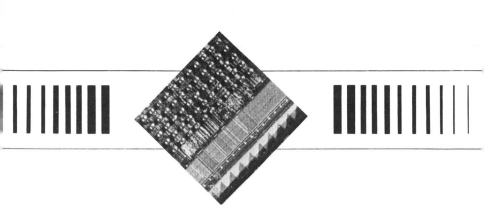

The Magic Chip

EXPLORING MICROELECTRONICS

Frank Ross, Jr.

Julian Messner  New York

Manufactured in the United States of America

10 9 8 7 6 5 4 3 2

Design by Howard B. Petlack, A Good Thing, Inc.

Library of Congress Cataloging in Publication Data.

Ross, Frank Xavier, 1914–
   The magic chip.

   Includes index.
   Summary: Traces the creation and development of one
of the greatest technological developments of the
twentieth century, the microchip, and describes some of
the electronic products and systems that owe their
existence to the chip
   1. Microelectronics—Juvenile literature. 2. Integrated circuits—Juvenile literature. [1. Microelectronics. 2. Electronics. 3. Technology] I. Title.
TK7874.R66   1984   621.3819'5835   84-10808
ISBN: 0-671-49373-6

*To my wife Laura in deepest gratitude
for her untiring assistance.*

Contents

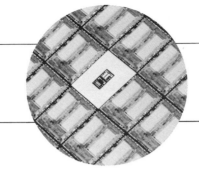

1

The Microchip

Smaller than a child's fingernail, the microchip is performing electronic magic in our homes, in industry, in medicine, indeed, in just about every area of our daily lives. It is the heart and brain of the extraordinary electronic products that are rapidly transforming almost all aspects of modern life. As a technological achievement and because of its impact on society, the chip must rank as one of the foremost laboratory creations of modern times.

How did this microscopic device come to be invented? Who was its originator? What makes it an

A microchip is tiny on the tip of a human finger. In the background is a greatly enlarged portion of the electronic circuits on the chip's surface. These electronic tracks enable a microchip to perform its wizardlike operations.

Courtesy ITT Semiconductors

important discovery? The answers to these questions make a story that covers many years and the patient labors of numerous dedicated scientists and engineers in a variety of technical fields. The quest finally reached a climax in the successful efforts of electronics engineers to develop the microchip. To appreciate what they did, we must first place the chip's invention in proper perspective to the rest of the evolving electronics field.

During World War II, scientists on both sides of the conflict constantly sought better weapons. Technicians in all areas, particularly electronics, worked feverishly toward that goal. One of their greatest discoveries was radar (*ra*dio *d*etection and *r*anging). This electronic eye, which is capable of seeing through blinding fog and in the darkness of night, helped to prevent Great Britain from collapsing under the crushing blows of the German Luftwaffe. Radar was largely a triumph of British scientists and engineers and undoubtedly the single most important electronic development to come out of World War II. It still performs vital services in a number of peacetime fields, principally commercial aviation.

In addition to radar, a variety of other electronic developments for the military were invented during World War II. Among them were devices for aiming artillery, submarine detection equipment, field communication systems, and complex equipment for fighter planes and bombers including automatic gun-firing apparatus, navigational aids, and electronic devices for precision bombing.

In the beginning of World War II, if a bomber plane had a radio and several electronic accessories for navigation, it was considered a modern, well-equipped aircraft. By the time that conflict ended in 1945, however, the newest bombers, such as the B-29 of the U.S. Air Force, were so packed with electronic gear that they could easily have served as airborne electronic laboratories. The complex electronic installations aboard the B-29, for example, had close to a thousand vacuum tubes and thousands of other passive electronic devices.

When the war ended, those working on the frontier of electronics research could glimpse great wonders ahead. Many of the recent developments were oriented toward military applications, but they also had great potential for peacetime uses. However, there was a general feeling among electronics scientists and engineers that before these future wonders could be attained, breakthroughs in theoretical knowledge and new technical developments had to be achieved. Conventional electronic devices had about reached their limits in design and function.

A particularly serious barrier blocking the way to more advanced electronic equipment was the long-used vacuum tube. Bulky, fragile, unreliable, and costly to produce, the tube was considered inadequate for the electronics of the future. The military in the United States, ever in search of better and deadlier fighting equipment, supported many postwar research and development projects that helped to bring about the desired theoretical and technical goals.

The National Aeronautics and Space Agency (NASA) was also involved with research and development in electronics in the 1950s and 1960s.

Charged with guiding U.S. space activities, NASA's scientists and engineers realized early that electronics had to play a critical role in the development of successful and practical spacecraft. Consequently, like the military, NASA became extremely active in supporting a number of different research programs that sought more advanced electronics.

This broad-ranging and vigorously conducted search for new electronics technology was also aided by private industry—particularly communications companies. Radio, television (beginning to boom in the fifties and sixties), and the telephone were moving toward new heights of development. But their technical progress was stymied by the existing electronic devices and equipment.

One area where the need for newer and better electronic technology was most apparent—indeed, most serious—was telephone communications. During the postwar decades the demands for telephone communications grew enormously. It was difficult to develop the necessary equipment to meet the mushrooming demand—to say nothing of adequately maintaining normal service. Researchers and technologists were hard-pressed to meet the technical challenge.

Out of this effort came the first big breakthrough in postwar electronics. The event took place in the Bell Telephone Laboratories in 1947 with the invention of the transistor. No bigger than a postage stamp, the transistor launched the revolutionary age of microelectronics.

The newly invented transistor was made public in 1948. Its makers described it as a point-contact transistor. The tiny device consisted of two sharp metal points, closely positioned and in touch with an N-type (negatively charged) crystal of germanium. The transistor's purpose was to amplify current.

Along with the negative charge of the transistor, positive charges were also present. Together, the two opposing charges produced active electronic effects. For the first time scientists had succeeded in creating amplification using a solid-state substance, that is, one that controls current without using heated filaments.

The germanium used in the first transistor is a material called a semiconductor. Semiconductor materials were no strangers to researchers, who were aware that a few substances under certain conditions had the ability to behave electrically. For example, at high temperatures they conduct current about as well as metals. When subjected to cold, the material loses its ability to conduct electricity and performs more like an insulator. By altering the crystal structure of semiconductor materials, scientists learned that their electrical properties could be changed. Germanium was used for the first transistor because it was the most easily obtainable semiconductor material in the required pure form. Silicon later took over as the principal material in nearly all transistors.

The transistor developed in 1947 was the result of a team effort by three research physicists working at Bell Labs—William Shockley, John Bardeen, and Walter H. Brattain. They had been guided to the newborn electronic device while conducting basic research in theoretical and experimental physics of solids, especially on the properties of semiconductor materials. The three inventors of the transistor were performing their research activities as part of a still larger laboratory program aimed at finding new and more efficient switching devices and amplifiers, key components in telephone communication systems. The glass-enclosed vacuum tubes were the workhorses for performing such tasks up to that time.

Although the first transistor was far from a finished product, it performed so well that its inventors felt they had created a device with enormous potential advantages over the vacuum tube. The transistor could detect, amplify, rectify (convert alternating current to direct current), and switch currents. Extremely small, rugged as compared with the glass vacuum tube, and less costly to manufacture, the transistor used little power and produced a relatively small amount of heat. The revolutionary invention was to prove the key that would unlock a treasure chest of electronic magic in the decades ahead.

After refinement, the point-contact transistor found its first useful applications in hearing aids and electronic switches in telephone communications. Most popular of all the early uses of the transistor was its employment in the pocket-size radio in 1954. Today, millions of these tiny transistors are in existence and serving as a replacement for the vacuum tube in a wide variety of electronic products.

Even though it was an invention of the utmost significance, the transistor languished for almost ten years before it was widely adopted by the electronics industry. The industry was reluctant to use the device mainly because it was difficult and expensive to make. For example, the transistor's pure crystal of semiconductor material was extremely expensive.

The industry's attitude changed when new techniques and materials made possible more efficient and less costly procedures for manufacturing transistors. Silicon rapidly replaced germanium as the semiconductor material, and today it is most commonly used.

If the engineers and technologists of the electronics industry were reluctant at first to accept the transistor, such was not the case with those in pure research. Physicists investigating solid-state semiconductor materials saw immediately that their colleagues at Bell Labs had scored a brilliant success—a success, incidentally, that brought the transistor's inventors the Nobel Prize in Physics in 1956. The invention stirred up the scientific community not only in the United States but in other countries as well. There was a sudden enthusiastic interest in semiconductors and their potential for bringing a brand-new world of electronics into existence.

An English physicist is generally credited by his fellow scientists with the original idea of using semiconductor technology to make a totally different kind of electronic device in miniature. The scientist was radar specialist G. W. A. Dummer of the Royal Radar Establishment. His idea was first expressed in print in 1952. Here is the kernel of his concept in part:

> With the advent of the transistor and the work in semiconductors generally, it seems now possible to envisage electronics equipment in a solid block with

16

no connecting wires. The block may consist of layers of insulating, conducting, rectifying and amplifying materials being connected directly by cutting out areas of the various layers.

Not too long after publication of this idea, other scientists and engineers, stimulated by the theoretical proposal, became involved with research to produce just such a device. Dummer's theoretical concept was in reality a blueprint for the next milestone in the development of microelectronics, the integrated circuit, or chip. Although he had not suggested the technical procedures for making such a device, Dummer had intrigued electronics engineers both overseas and in this country. A kind of international competition soon got under way that had as its goal the creation of this much-to-be-desired device. All who participated knew the prize would be lucrative. But just how lucrative the participants did not even faintly guess.

Dummer's pioneering concept for an integrated circuit caught the attention of a youthful American electronics engineer, Jack S. Kilby. Fresh out of the University of Illinois in 1947 with a degree in electrical engineering, Kilby began his career with an electronics firm called Centralab. His assignments included designing and developing miniature electronic components for use in hearing aids.

Eventually Kilby began to make transistors and incorporate them into the various products manufactured at Centralab under license from Bell Labs. To stimulate the use of their invention, Bell Labs freely licensed the production of the solid-state device to companies that were interested.

Kilby worked for several years at Centralab, a period that served as training for his major engineering achievement. Working primarily with semiconductor materials like germanium, exploring new ways to make and adapt tiny transistors to electronic products provided an excellent outlet for his lively technical mind.

In the spring of 1958, feeling that he had gone as far as he could at Centralab, Kilby quit. By this time, original ideas about solid-state semiconductor devices were crowding his mind. The young engineer decided that the company's technical facilities and financial resources would not permit him to develop his ideas to their fullest. Research and development are extremely costly.

In May 1958 Kilby joined Texas Instruments, a thriving electronics firm concerned almost exclusively with the development and manufacture of semiconductor devices—transistors, resistors, and capacitors. Texas Instruments turned Kilby loose in the department concerned with the microminiaturization of electronic components. This was greatly to his liking, and he plunged into his work with enthusiasm.

The first task given the young engineer was to design an amplifier and squeeze it into the smallest package possible. Technically, Kilby met his first challenge successfully. However, the electronic device was too expensive to produce.

The disappointing result of his first assignment left Kilby discouraged. He was afraid that the company would transfer him to another department if he couldn't come up with a more cost-efficient design. That would have been a setback to his career. His present position placed him in the front line of semiconductor development work, exactly where he most wanted to be.

Returning to his original design, Kilby thought deeply on ways of making it more cost efficient. Then a thought came to him: Texas Instruments was making profits as a manufacturer of semiconductors, so why shouldn't it concentrate on these solid-state devices for his design? Furthermore, why couldn't the company make the entire circuit according to his semiconductor design, since this was the only kind that the unit really needed? The less active components, resistors, and capacitors, for example, could be made from the same material as the more active elements to be used in the amplifier.

As the idea expanded in Kilby's mind, his discouragement gave way to rising enthusiasm. One other thought came to the engineer. Since all the components of his proposed new design were to made of a single material, they could also be made as a single unit interconnected to form a complete circuit. Kilby, perhaps not fully aware of it at the time, was almost within reach of the complete semiconductor circuit concept described by Dummer some years earlier.

The young electronics engineer went to his drawing board where he spent long hours working out the features of his novel circuit design. When he was finally satisfied, he showed the results to his boss who was deeply interested but who had some reservations. Would Kilby's design work? This was a question that only a working model could answer. So the boss suggested that Kilby build one.

Losing little time, Kilby began constructing his revolutionary circuit. He used discrete, single-function silicon devices—transistors, resistors, and capacitors. He obtained the electronic value of these devices by etching away excess silicon. Finally, the rudimentary semiconductor circuit was assembled and ready for a demonstration on August 28, 1958. To the great satisfaction of its inventor and his boss, the test was successful. It showed that a complete electronic circuit could be constructed using only semiconductor elements.

Although Kilby's semiconductor was an enormously significant advance in electronics, the invention fell short of his original conception. To make his pioneering semiconductor unit work, the young engineer had been forced to change the assembly so that it was not a wholly integrated circuit. Parts necessary for that were not available. Electronic technology had not yet caught up with theory. But the goal of an integrated circuit was almost within Kilby's reach, and now, greatly encouraged, he began a new round of work to achieve it.

Using electronic elements newly developed by other engineers at Texas Instruments—a diffused wafer less than ½ inch square was one—Kilby went about building his circuit. This was to be an electronic hookup known as a phase-shift oscillator. The wafer of germanium was sliced into bars $\frac{1}{16}$ inch wide by almost ½ inch long. This formed the base of the circuit and would also be involved with the latter's electronic action. The circuit was laid out on the bar with the necessary interconnections between the unit's components and the base. The result was a unified single structure. No wires were employed as with a conventional electronic circuit.

By September 12, 1958, Kilby was ready to test his new brainchild. Before three colleagues including his boss, he applied power to the oscillator. It worked, and Kilby's colleagues warmly congratulated him. The invention was to prove enormously significant, not only for Texas Instruments but also for the entire field of electronics. Kilby had put Dummer's theory into action. He then took steps to patent the integrated circuit in January of 1959. At first he called it the solid circuit because it was made of solid-state materials and devices. At a later point in its development the integrated circuit acquired its more popular name—the chip.

Kilby wanted to demonstrate that the solid circuit was not limited in its application to just certain types of electronic circuits but could be used for a number of different kinds including those for digital functions. To do this, Kilby and his associates went on to build and demonstrate several different types.

Now Texas Instruments realized the importance of Kilby's creation and gave him support in continuing to develop his invention. The company even went to the extent of dropping its other microminiature products and concentrating on moving the integrated circuit from the laboratory to the marketplace. The company's leaders could see an extremely valuable use for the new invention in future electronic equipment and products.

While Texas Instruments was busily clearing its decks for future electronic manufacturing with emphasis on the integrated circuit, Kilby continued to refine and improve his invention. He was instrumen-

This crude-looking device was an early experimental integrated circuit invented at Texas Instruments.

Courtesy Texas Instruments, Inc.

tal in making better capacitors and resistors, and he helped develop techniques for packaging the semiconductor unit. This effort resulted in fitting all the needed components into a flat pack that measured ⅛ inch by ¼ inch, thus establishing a standard that became nearly universal in the future mass production of the integrated circuit, or chip. Also vital to this developing activity were Kilby's contributions to better manufacturing methods of the circuit's various components.

Satisfied at having brought the integrated circuit to the point of production and practical application, Texas Instruments revealed the existence of the revolutionary electronic device to the public on March 6, 1959. This took place at an electronics technical show held in New York City. The company announcement said in part that the solid-state semiconductor integrated circuit was the most significant technical development since the creation and commercial availability of the transistor in 1954.

Texas Instruments strongly believed that applications of Kilby's invention would at first be useful for the further miniaturizing of electronic computers; these would be used for military equipment: devices to guide missiles and compact electronic equipment for use aboard fighter aircaft. In a longer-range view, Texas Instruments saw the integrated circuit's usefulness in making smaller and more reliable consumer products such as radios and television sets. The prophetic accuracy of Texas Instruments is evident today in the bewildering number and variety of electronic products and processes that in large part owe their existence to the integrated circuit, or chip.

Revelation of the integrated circuit aroused considerable interest among electronic engineers, not only at the New York show but also throughout the country. Many were skeptical about the device and voiced their doubts. Circuits of the integrated, semiconductor type were difficult if not impossible to mass produce. Their production would be extremely costly. Another objection was that electronic circuits of this kind would be expensive and extremely difficult to repair.

Despite these questions as the decade of the sixties began, semiconductor development continued at an ever faster pace. Integrated circuits, related components and devices, and manufacturing techniques all experienced rapid change. By the midpoint of the decade the transistor, the integrated circuit, and other new electronic devices were being produced and adapted to many different kinds of electronic products and equipment. The reservations that many technical people had concerning the integrated circuit quietly disappeared.

First put into production by Texas Instruments in 1962, the solid-state semiconductor was produced in ever increasing volume thereafter as manufacturers of electronic products saw the great advantages in using the chip. It not only helped to reduce the size of products and equipment, like computers, but more important, it also eliminated the excessively high cost of building complex electronic circuits using wired interconnections.

The sixties and seventies were tumultuous years for the microelectronics industry, which grew by leaps and bounds. Many new companies were established by young, bright, ambitious electronics engineers eager to climb aboard the microelectronics bandwagon. They, too, made scores of technical contributions that gave a strong boost to the growing high-technology industry. Although they directed much of their attention to making more powerful and efficient integrated circuits, they also placed a great deal of emphasis on finding ways to produce the miniature device efficiently and at the lowest possible cost. The Planar Process, which resulted from this research, became one of the major manufacturing techniques used by the semiconductor industry.

One technical event was to have a great influence on the development and use of the chip: the invention of the microprocessor in 1971. Once again, an extraordinary microelectronics device was developed by a group of young engineers working for an equally young firm, the Intel Company, which was little more than ten years old. It was founded by several young engineers led by Robert Noyce, formerly associated with Fairchild Semiconductor. Noyce made such important improvements in the basic design of the integrated circuit that he is sometimes considered the creator of the device.

The chip was a major milestone in the establishment and growth of the microelectronics industry. Extraordinary products and equipment—computers, pocket calculators, multipurpose telephones, and others—have been made available to a public bewildered by their dazzling performance. To this day there is no sign of a letup in this outpouring of technological magic.

Those involved in the technical development

areas of the microelectronics industry like to para-phrase the words of the circus ringmaster, "You haven't seen anything yet." The technology they say is truly only on the threshold of even more amazing achievements to come over the next fifty years.

2

How Chips Are Made

This century, which will soon end, included the motor age, the jazz age, the postwar era, the nuclear age, the space age, and now the computer age. The last name recognizes the variety and extraordinary number of computers used in our society. More important, perhaps, is the impact they are having on our everyday activities.

Computers have become indispensable because of a single electronic device, the magic chip. Although smaller than a child's fingernail, the microchip is considered one of the outstanding technological triumphs of our century. This conclusion is based not only on the seemingly magical performance of the tiny unit but also on the extraordinarily complex processes involved in its manufacture.

The chip is aptly named. Today's common variety measures about ¼ inch on each side and is thinner than an ordinary piece of corrugated cardboard. The manufacturing processes used in creating chips are highly complex and unusual. The work area must be spotless and as dustless as possible. It must be as clean as a hospital operating room. The "clean room" is essential since a single speck of dust can render a chip useless. To help create this superclean environment the air of the work area is continuously filtered and workers wear gowns and head coverings like surgeons.

Once the science behind the creation of a chip was worked out, not an easy task, it was no less difficult to develop the necessary processes for its practical and economic manufacture.

Most chips in use today are made of the semiconductor material called silicon. A few consist of germanium or gallium. These are natural substances with electrical qualities and can be altered either to conduct a charge or to be nonconductive. They are classed as semiconductors and are found in their natural state in large quantities. Silicon is certainly a common enough substance since it is what sand is made of.

Silicon at the moment is the preferred base material for making chips, mainly because it responds readily to processes that give it conducting or nonconducting properties. Also, because it is so common, silicon is readily available at a reasonable cost.

Because the tiniest dust particle can damage an integrated circuit during manufacture, the chips are processed in virtually dust-free chambers, commonly known as "clean rooms." In a clean room, air streams constantly from ceiling to floor to force any dust in the air through the floor's tiny holes. Also, people who work in a clean room are required to wear paper head coverings, rubber gloves, lab coats, and, in some cases, shoe coverings to ensure that they do not transmit any dust to the chips they process.

Courtesy Bell Laboratories

Obviously, the silicon, or sand, cannot be used directly as it comes from a source. It must be processed to enhance its electrical properties and to put it into a form suitable for use in manufacturing. A fluid chemical mixture is made from the silicon so that the end product is a solid mass of 99.90 percent pure crystalline silicon. The solid mass of silicon crystal is in the form of a cylinder four inches in diameter and about three feet long.

Paper-thin wafers are cut from the log, the way a butcher cuts slices from a length of bologna. Because the material is very hard and the cut must be precise, a diamond-cutting tool is used for this step. The wafers are then subjected to a series of procedures that ultimately transform them into electrically correct chips.

The first step is to place large numbers of wafers on sliding racks, which are then pushed into long, cylindrical ovens. These ovens are heated to a temperature of almost 2,000 degrees Fahrenheit. The ovens are also filled with a gas highly saturated with oxygen or simple steam.

This process coats the wafer surfaces with an extremely thin layer of silicon dioxide. This coating is much like the rust that forms on a metal pipe. The layer is designed to prevent short circuits within the electrical circuits that eventually are to be imprinted on the chips.

Next, the wafer is infused with the correct electronic characteristics both on its surface and within the material. Some of the processes involved at this stage include ion implantation, electron beam bombardment, and X-rays.

Wafers are then given another chemical coat; this layer is photo-resist. It is an emulsion substance commonly used in photographic processes for screening out light.

Following this step the wafers are ready to be imprinted with electronic circuits, the first of the procedures that will transform the semiconductor material into a microchip.

The circuits are imprinted on the surface of the wafer by means of masks. These are full-scale drawings made by circuit designers on plastic sheets about three feet wide. The circuits determine the microchip's ultimate functions in computers, microprocessors, and other equipment.

The large masks, of course, cannot be used to transfer the circuit onto the wafer. They must first be photographically reduced. Scaled down to proper size, the first of the masks is laid over the wafer. The miniature mask contains hundreds of identical copies of a circuit pattern. This is only one of several layers that will ultimately be photoetched onto the wafer's surface.

After it is placed over the surface of a chip layer, a mask is bathed in ultraviolet light. This imprints the circuit pattern onto the light-sensitive surface. Those portions of the pattern exposed to the light harden and form an outline of the circuit. The parts of the chip layer shielded from the light by the mask remain soft and are eventually washed away in an acid bath. A number of different patterns on separate layers may be imprinted in this manner until a chip is considered finished.

Following this photolith step the wafers are put on

MAKING MICROCHIPS

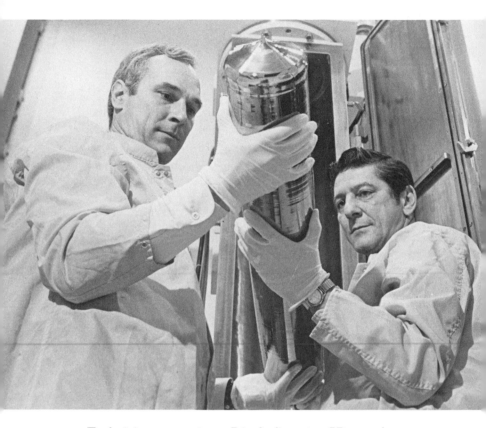

Technicians removing a 5 inch diameter, 55-pound cylinder of silicon from a crystal "growing" chamber. Grown from pure silicon under computer control, the silicon is melted in a glass crucible at 2680 degrees Fahrenheit. A rotating "seed" of silicon is dipped into the molten mass and slowly pulled out to form the crystal cylinder. The process takes twenty-four hours. A cylinder of such size can be sliced into nine hundred razor-thin wafers. Each wafer can contain five hundred chips and each chip can contain 1,500 computer logic circuits.

Courtesy IBM Corporation

Razor-thin wafers are sliced from a silicon crystal cylinder.

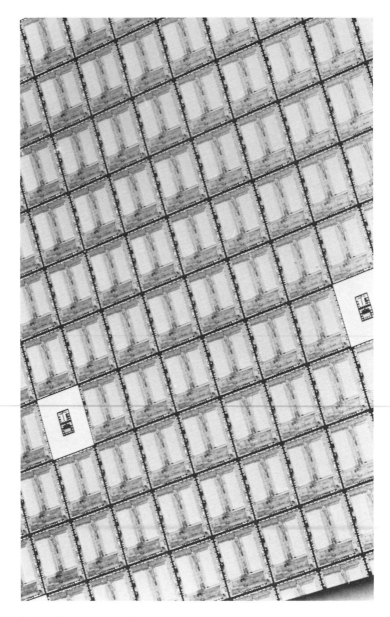

Part of a silicon wafer containing several hundred chips.
Courtesy ITT Semiconductors

Circular discs are wafers of silicon, each containing twenty-nine circuit chips. Each chip has 36,000 transistors. The photo shows the chips in one phase of their manufacture.

This Bell Laboratories engineer is holding a silicon wafer containing sixty-four microcomputer chips. A small portion of one chip appears enlarged four hundred times on the video monitor in the background.

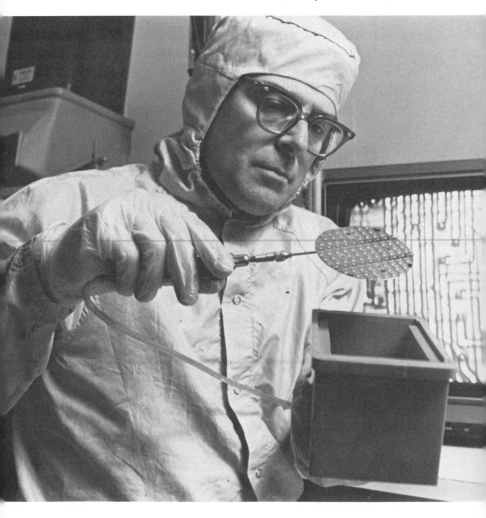

The silicon wafer being shown holds a number of experimental chips. The insert upper left is a portion of the same wafer magnified about five hundred times. "A" shows a capacitor and "B" a pair of transistors. Ongoing experiments such as this seek to make chips with a greater memory capacity and speed of operation among other features.

Courtesy IBM Corporation

the racks again and slid back into the cylindrical superhot ovens. This time the air within the oven is filled with special gases saturated with "dopants." These are microscopic impurities that give the microchip a particular electronic characteristic. If the impurities reduce the electron population, on an area of the chip, it becomes an electrically positive, or P, section. If the neighboring area receives an excess of electrons, it becomes a negative, or N, section.

When two N sections are divided by a P section, they act as a transistor, an amplifier of current. This is also referred to as an electronic switch.

The N and P sections acting together in each layer form transistors, resistors, for controlling the flow of current, or capacitors. The capacitors store current. The fluctuations in an electronic current flowing between the N zones is controlled by a small voltage in the P zone. This arrangement permits thousands of microscopic transistors, or electronic switches, to be installed on a single tiny silicon chip.

In the second baking process the chemical impurities diffuse into the solid silicon material.

In the final phase of manufacture the whole wafer is covered with an aluminium conductor for interconnecting the circuits. This phase also involves a series of processes of masking, etching, and acid bathing.

The wafer is then subjected to close inspection for defects. This is done with the help of a computerized electron-scanning microscope that minutely examines the wafer for faulty circuits and marks the defective chips in red. Technicians use a diamond cutter to score the wafer in a grid pattern, enabling each individual microchip to be snapped free. A single wafer can produce more than 250 microchips, each about ¼ inch square.

The defective chips are thrown out; the good ones are externally wired, sealed in a plastic or metallic protective coat, and shipped.

The mass production of microchips involves extremely complex manufacturing procedures. Despite this, the individual cost of a chip is pennies. This compares with the dollar cost of a chip during the early years of its existence in the late 1950s and 1960s.

Under a microscope the microchip looks like a Navajo rug. Some scientists compare its pattern to that of a railroad switching yard or to the maze puzzles that were popular some years ago. These re-

This experimental chip, only ⅜ inch long, is shown on a magnified portion of the Declaration of Independence. The chip can store 288,000 bits of data. Chips with double that capacity are now in the development stage.

Courtesy IBM Corporation

quired a puzzle solver to trace a path through a series of alleyways, starting from the outer edge and working toward the center. The mazes in these puzzles, however, were in one dimension only. The maze, or circuitry, of a chip is in two dimensions. In addition to its surface, it also has depth.

The first chips made in 1959 for commercial use were not very "smart" compared with those being made today. In fact, the early chips held only a single "bit" of information, or data. As engineers became

expert at improving this magic device, however, the chip's "brain" power was increased to about 1,000 "bits" in 1970 and then skyrocketed to 32,000 six years later. In 1983 a new chip was unveiled that contained more than 500,000 bits of data for faster, more powerful, more versatile computers.

A computer is being used to help design new, more efficient integrated circuits.

Courtesy Bell Laboratories

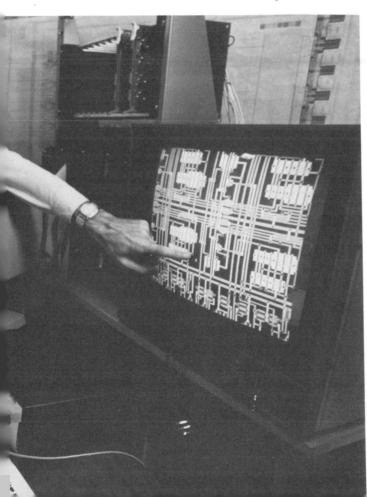

The newer, more powerful chips were also identified differently. Some were known as large-scale integrated circuits (LSI); others more powerful still were called very large scale integrated circuits (VLSI).

All the magic qualities given the microchip have been the work of youthful, brilliant electronics scientists and engineers. Most of the inventors of the transistor—Kilby who brought into existence the integrated circuit; M. D. Hoff, creator of the microprocessor; and a host of other pioneers—were men in their twenties or thirties. Youth was the name of the game at the start of the microchip industry more than thirty years ago, and young scientists are still the leaders in this field. Indeed, the entire field of microelectronics from chip manufacturing to the production of computers and all the auxiliary electronic products, is dominated by young professionals.

The youthfulness of microelectronics was largely responsible for yet another development in the field. This was the proliferation of new businesses conducting research, development, and manufacturing of the microchip and many other microelectronic components. Spurred on by ambition and dreams of financial success, new electronics companies sprouted like mushrooms in California, Texas, New England, and Long Island, New York.

Combining technical knowledge with a keen business sense, many of these youthful entrepreneurs became millionaires. Some few went on to become multimillionaires. Not all were that successful, of course.

The semiconductor industry had its beginning in the 1950s. William Shockley, one of the trio who brought the transistor into existence, left Bell Labs at that time to start his own company, Shockley Transistor Corporation, in Palo Alto, California. From this seminal enterprise dozens of other semiconductor companies eventually sprouted.

Shockley's company had not been in existence much more than a year when it was jolted by the departure of eight of its top-flight engineers. They saw the enormous potential of the semiconductor in practical applications and the equally enormous financial gain to be had. The engineers chose to gamble their knowledge and skills in the marketplace.

Supported financially by Fairchild Camera and Instrument Corporation the eight engineers established the Fairchild Semiconductor Company. Success greeted their efforts from the very beginning. The company grew increasingly profitable as the entire industry accelerated at an astonishing rate.

But Fairchild Semiconductor experienced some bumps on the joy ride to success. As fast as new engineers were added to the staff a number of veteran engineers left. Their reasons were similar to those of dozens of other engineers—not unhappiness with company policies or practices, but dreams of establishing their own semiconductor firms.

Nearly all the Fairchild graduates were successful, and one new company after another showed robust black figures on the profit side of its ledgers. The fledgling enterprises became involved with all aspects of the burgeoning high-technology industry, from silicon wafers and microchips to computers and computer software.

Outstanding among the companies established by former Fairchild employees is the Intel Corporation, mentioned in the first chapter. Robert Noyce

A computer-controlled laser beam is used to transform defective memory chips into good ones.

and Gordon Moore were the chief founders of this concern, which today is one of the largest microchip manufacturers in the world. As noted earlier Noyce, the brilliant scientist and engineer, had long been involved with research and development of the integrated circuit. Shortly after Kilby revealed his invention of the integrated circuit, Noyce made some significant contributions of his own to the device.

As we have seen, young professionals dominated the semiconductor industry during its teething period in the early and mid-1950s. Today, youth is still the kingpin of this now giant industrial field. The affinity between youth and microelectronics is hard to explain. It may be due to the fact that the technology itself is quite young and thus appeals to young people. Or it could also be the complex nature of microelectronics that intrigues the alert, inquisitive minds of the young. They are fascinated by the complicated world of the magic chip and they have mastered it.

Be that as it may, the opportunities for fame and fortune are still available in the semiconductor industry. And young people today, as in the earlier years of microchip production, continue to involve themselves in that activity in search of the elusive pot of gold.

Although the following words were written in *Scientific American* by Robert N. Noyce in the late 1970s, they have as much application now as they did then:

> The microelectronics revolution is far from having run its course. We are still learning how to exploit the potential of the integrated circuit by developing

new theories and designing new circuits whose performance may yet be improved by another order of magnitude.

And so the semiconductor industry still dangles its lures to attract youthful electronics engineers and technicians. There is no end of candidates who plan to go into the business of microelectronics for themselves. For example, the owner of Double-Gold Software, Jeff Gold, is still in his early twenties, yet he is the originator of a software computer program that secures computer information from theft. The youthful electronics and computer wizard has successfully marketed his product throughout the world. This program and Jeff Gold's other electronic ideas promise soon to put him into the multimillion dollar club. There are numerous others like him.

Despite its youthfulness the semiconductor business and indeed the whole microelectronics field has mushroomed into a giant multibillion dollar industry in little more than three decades. It is now ranked along with the other three giants of America's industrial might—automobile manufacturing, steel making, and chemicals production.

Three factors helped to stimulate the phenomenal growth of the semiconductor industry: the U.S. Defense Department's demand for electronic components to support its growing array of complex electronic equipment; the needs of a modernizing telecommunications industry; and the rapidly expanding consumer products market. And much of this ballooning industrial activity, largely occurring throughout the 1960s and 1970s, took place in the Santa Clara valley of California.

After William Shockley set up his transistor plant in Palo Alto, others quickly followed, establishing plants up and down the valley. Located in a lush agricultural area south of San Francisco, the region today is dotted with hundreds of semiconductor and other microelectronic plants.

Magic chips and their constant technical improvement into ever more powerful and versatile microelectronic devices dominate the beehive activity of the area, which is known as Silicon Valley. The valley is the heart of the semiconductor business in the United States, but other regions are well populated by such plants, too. These include Long Island, the area along Route 128 near Boston, and Dallas, where the giant semiconductor company Texas Instruments has its headquarters.

Silicon Valley's independently owned semiconductor businesses with names like Signetica, Intel, and Advanced Micro Devices are fiercely competitive. Each strives to obtain the best engineers available by offering extraordinary salaries and fringe benefits. In this way they hope to produce a better chip or related semiconductor product than their neighboring competitors can offer.

Many believe that this intense rivalry has kept the microelectronic field in a continuous state of advancement. As chips were improved in memory capacity and logic, new uses were found for them in a bewildering variety of products. These have poured out of the factories with great rapidity over the past two decades.

At any rate, as the American semiconductor and related microelectronics businesses hummed along at full speed, they enjoyed a near total monopoly in the marketplace, both at home and throughout the world. But these glory years, more than twenty-five of them, were bound to end one day. Scientists and electronics engineers in other lands were also eager to get a piece of the microchip business. This was especially true of the technically proficient Japanese. Just as they did in the business of producing television sets and automobiles, Japanese technologists and manufacturers are giving the U.S. semiconductor industry a stiff run for market supremacy.

Japan's industrial might today represents an extraordinary success story. Rising from the ashes of war devastation, including the horrors of two atomic bomb attacks, Japan through the post–World War II years has advanced with astonishing swiftness into the ranks of the industrial giants. It is now rubbing elbows with the United States.

Japan's achievements have been due in part to skilled technologists, a dedicated labor force, and shrewd business ability. Working together as a unit these elements have helped to create an industrial empire that has caused unprecedented repercussions in other industrial nations, but principally the United States.

The Japanese built their industrial empire on the unique ability to take a product developed elsewhere, refine it to improve its functions, and then manufacture the product under more efficient processes for less cost. As a result, they have been able to make deep inroads in the world markets with better and cheaper products.

The Japanese, long before the war, displayed talent for copying a product made elsewhere and then swamping a market at far below the product's original cost. But they presented no threat during the prewar years. Their products were generally shoddy in workmanship and found few buyers. In fact, this characteristic of Japanese-made goods became so notorious that the label "Made in Japan" almost turned into a synonym for "trash."

That state of affairs is far from true today, however. Japanese products are well designed and excellently constructed. They are no longer spurned but are in fact eagerly sought by buyers in countries the world over. Since the United States is the topmost marketplace in the world, Japanese industrialists zeroed in on us with special attention.

To see how effective they have been one need only talk to TV makers and auto manufacturers in this country. Both have felt the full impact of the Japanese commercial onslaught. The U.S. television industry has been all but wiped out. Those few American companies still in the field have moved their factories to foreign lands where cheaper labor is available.

U.S. car manufacturers have been sent reeling by the massive invasion of compact and midcompact Japanese autos. Americans have been buying them by the thousands, not only because these vehicles fill a size need but also because of their sound construction, lower selling price, and more economical operating costs.

Now the semiconductor industry in this country is bracing for the Japanese competition. One American chip manufacturer has characterized it as "war."

In the early 1970s the American makers of the magic chip started to feel the Japanese competition.

By the middle and later years of that decade the Japanese manufacturers of chips and other microelectronic components and products—pocket calculators and desktop computers, for example—were becoming formidable opponents in the marketplace. Many Silicon Valley magic chip people were disturbed and even angered by the character of the intensifying competition.

The Japanese at first did little basic research relating to the transistor, integrated circuit, and all the other startling microelectronic devices that launched the present revolutionary high-technology electronic industry. They were also lacking in knowledge concerning the manufacturing processes needed to make semiconductors on a mass basis and at reasonable cost. These were strictly American scientific and engineering accomplishments.

A gap of some ten years separated the Japanese technologists from the frontier in microelectronics that had been established in the United States. In order to close this gap and add the semiconductor business to their other postwar industrial and economic achievements, the Japanese embarked on a massive catch-up drive. Their goal was a share—the lion's share if possible—of not only the business of developing new and more powerful chips but also of microelectronic consumer products and computers. The sum total of this microelectronic industrial activity was reckoned in the multibillions of dollars. This was the size of the microelectronics plum by the early 1980s.

Interestingly enough when the Japanese began their vigorous catch-up efforts, the Silicon Valley

New fabrication techniques for very large scale integrated circuits are tested by making standard test chips then measuring the passage of known currents through them. The photo shows a prober measuring the current.

Courtesy Bell Laboratories

people were generous about letting them see their laboratories and production facilities. In this way an unending stream of technical information flowed from the United States to Japan.

Applying their undisputed skill at copying and refining, the Japanese were soon turning out microchips and other products that were on a par with and often superior to the American varieties. By the middle and late 1970s semiconductor and microelectronic products manufacturers in America began to realize that the Japanese were encroaching on their nearly exclusive world market. Most important, this erosion was even eating away the home market where, since the beginnings of the microchip business in the 1950s, American manufacturers held total sway. By the mid-1970s Japanese rivalry had begun to reach serious proportions.

The American semiconductor manufacturers, in the Silicon Valley and elsewhere in the United States did an about-face in their attitude toward the Japanese. No longer do they open their laboratory and manufacturing plant doors to their Far East rivals. They now keep a tight lid on their research and development of new and more powerful microchips and on all improvements in manufacturing processes.

A factor that has aggravated the entire situation has been the policy among Japanese semiconductor manufacturers of maintaining tight security on their own research and manufacturing advances. Americans who attempted to see the latest Japanese research and development activities in microelectronics were almost always told there was nothing of importance behind the closed doors or that the work was unrelated to the microchip.

This attitude on the part of Japanese was enough to make the Americans feel resentful after years of freely giving access to their store of technological information. A further irritant, also intense, was the series of obstacles erected by the Japanese government to prevent U.S. manufacturers from selling their products in Japan.

This lack of reciprocity in the technical and commercial arenas has seriously affected overall trade relations between the two nations. The battle royal has now intensified to the point where more than private industry is involved. The two governments are deeply engaged in trying to work out an agreeable solution.

After Japanese engineers and other representatives of their microchip industry were barred from free entry into the citadels of Silicon Valley, they resorted to other tactics. So intent were they on obtaining the very latest technological data, especially about the future generation of microchips, that they used tactics both fair and foul.

Sadly, their unscrupulous efforts included bribery, paying large sums of money to U.S. microelectronic engineers for information about their research work. They also resorted to theft. U.S. officials have cracked down on technology thieves, however. Two representatives of the Japanese microconductor industry were recently found guilty in a trial in California, and seven other employees had charges against them dropped when they agreed to obey the law in the future.

As far as the Japanese are concerned, all this research and development unpleasantness may come to an end in the near future. Building on their existing research, the Japanese semiconductor industry and government have combined forces on a $200 million program to make their country undisputed leader in the field.

Based on their past industrial and commercial achievements, the Japanese could readily achieve their goal. To counter this threat, parts of the American semiconductor industry have banded together for the purpose of pooling finances and research to promote microchip knowledge. They are also lobbying to obtain government assistance in the competitive battle. Semiconductor people would like to see the U.S. government provide some of the funds for research, which is very costly, and to pass laws that would slow down the torrent of imported Japanese microelectronic products into this country. At the very least, they would like to see a deal arranged whereby the Japanese would allow more American imports into their market.

Semiconductor and microelectronics manufacturers feel that Uncle Sam has a large stake in the outcome of this struggle. It is essential, as they see it, that this country maintain a technologically and financially strong microelectronics industry, if for no other reason than for the nation's defense. Microelectronic products play a vital role in effective operation of all sorts of military weapons today. This part promises to be even greater tomorrow, especially if the world military establishments continue preparations for space-age warfare.

While the clang and clamor of the microchip marketplace is raging, the electronic wizards in this country, and increasingly in other nations, are quietly advancing the semiconductor field to new frontiers of technical accomplishment. With the plans for new, more powerful, and more versatile microchips springing from the scientists' ingenious minds, the microelectronics revolution we are currently experiencing promises to keep moving in high gear and to amaze us with its magic.

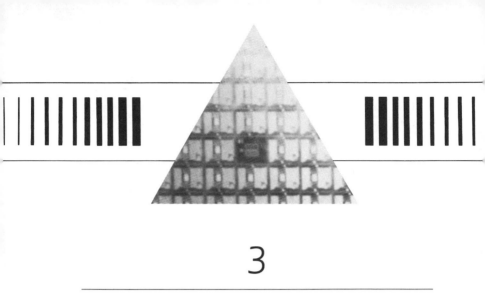

3

The Chip and the Computer

The pervasive presence of the computer in our modern society has come about primarily through the existence of that tiny, magical electronic device called the microchip. The integration of the two—the chip and the computer—has resulted in one of the most extraordinary and profoundly significant technological achievements of the twentieth century.

Before the electronic part of the computer's makeup evolved, the computer itself had been in existence for more than a hundred years. During its earliest period the computer was totally mechanical in its operation.

As science and technology advanced throughout the nineteenth century, the mechanical computer progressed to an electromechanical nature. Following that came the truly startling technical innovations that transformed the computer into a fully electronic machine with wizardlike performance abilities.

To repeat, the computer basically is a very old technical creation. As its name implies, it is a machine intended for handling numbers—adding, subtracting, and the like. We could actually trace its roots back to the dim, distant past in China, before the Christian era, where a simplified mechanical computer, the abacus, originated. Interestingly enough this mechanical counting device, a surprisingly effective performer, is still widely used in parts of Russia and the Far East. Sometimes it is used in schools in this country, too.

However, we need not go back quite that far to establish the lineage of the computer. It is sufficient for our story to pick up the threads in the seventeenth century. And since there were so many people involved with its creation, we shall mention only a few—scientists, mathematicians, and other thinkers who contributed most significantly to bringing the machine into existence.

Among the first of these was Blaise Pascal (1623–1662), a French physicist, student of religion, mathematician, and inventor of scientific devices. Pascal built a counting machine he called the Pascaline in the 1640s.

A brilliant mathematician, Pascal devised his mechanical creation to help his father, who worked for the government on tax business. As we all know, taxes and calculations are inseparable.

With the use of his son's Pascaline the elder Pascal found it easier and quicker to do the endless adding and subtracting that his work required. Science historians consider Pascal's invention the first major step toward a practical mechanical calculating machine.

We next come to a contemporary of Pascal's, Gottfried Wilhelm Leibniz (1646–1716). A German, Leibniz was also an intellectual whiz in a number of fields including philosophy, law, history, and, his first love, science. He was fascinated with Pascal's calculating machine, and being an inventor of sorts himself as well as a mathematician, he saw ways of improving the Frenchman's invention.

He changed the design of several of the gears within Pascal's calculator so that the machine could handle a whole series of arithmetical functions a great deal faster.

Leibniz's major mechanical contribution was a cylindrical drum filled with unique gears having teeth of different lengths. The German inventor's modifications were so effective that in one form or another they could be found in mechanical calculators for the next several hundred years.

Later, Leibniz concentrated on mathematics and worked out some of the early principles of the binary numerical system, which uses only the digits 0 and 1. This numerical language, after considerable refining, was eventually adapted for today's high-speed electronic computers. Indeed, if the binary system had not come into use and the decimal numerical arrangement employed, the scintillating performance of the current breed of computers would hardly be possible.

A man who stood head and shoulders above the rest of the computer pioneers was Charles Babbage (1792–1871). An Englishman, Babbage was a first-rate mathematician and an inventor. Among his many inventions was the cowcatcher, a gratelike unit attached to the front end of a steam locomotive. During the early years of railroading this device was important for nudging aside cattle that had strayed onto the tracks.

Independently wealthy, Babbage was a bit of a crank when it came to sloppiness in mathematical calculations. It upset him to encounter errors, especially in long tables of figures such as logarithms. But Babbage also realized that human failure was inevitable where endless repetition of figures was concerned.

Thinking long and hard about the problem, the English inventor conceived of a machine that could handle the problem and that would be far less prone to errors than humans were.

After working out the principles of his machine, which he called the Difference Engine, Babbage set about building it. However, he wasn't very far into his project before he was overwhelmed by other ideas for a vastly more advanced mechanical calculator. He junked his unfinished Difference Engine and plunged furiously into the task of working out the principles of his new machine, which he named the Analytical Engine.

It was a remarkable conception for its time. Powered by steam, Babbage's calculator was designed to be programmed to perform specific mathematical functions. Its principal job of calculating was to be done by a special unit called the mill. It also had a memory unit, an input unit, and a unit for controlling the machine. Finally, to take care of the calculator's output of streams of figures, there was a printing device. All of these parts sound very familiar to those who work with modern computers.

In order for his Analytical Engine to work properly, particularly the input and control features, Babbage used coded punched cards. These cards were invented in 1801 by the Frenchman Joseph Jacquard (1752–1834) for use with the looms on which silk was woven. Together with other mechanical innovations to the loom, Jacquard had revolutionized the silk-weaving industry in France. His inventions reduced the cost of silk weaving mainly by eliminating much of the human labor previously needed. As a consequence, he also brought the wrath of the working people down on his head. Babbage was the first to use punched cards for mathematical purposes, and they have been used in calculators and computers ever since, right down to the present day.

Babbage worked on his Analytical Engine for forty years. He used up almost all of his personal fortune in the long but vain effort. Even grants of money from the British government, which was interested in having the calculator perfected, were consumed in the project.

The problem that ultimately stymied Babbage was technological. His ideas for the various intricate components of the Analytical Engine were far in advance of what technology in his day could provide. For one thing, the precision required for the engine's many parts simply could not be achieved.

Modern computer experts who studied Babbage's plans for the Analytical Engine could find little wrong with his theoretical ideas. Many of these, in fact, like the memory and input units, became vital basic parts of present-day electronic computers. Despite his failure and because his concepts of a workable calculator anticipated many of the features of similar machines today, he is often referred to as the father of the computer.

After Charles Babbage the parade of pioneers who contributed to the evolution of the computer continued. And as the nineteenth century drew to a close, pioneers were at work in America as well as in Europe. Indeed, some of the more significant advances now took place in the United States.

Among these pioneers was Dorr Felt (1862–1930), who devised the first system employing keys to be punched for calculating numbers. With one swoop he eliminated the need to move levers or turn handles to operate the computer. Needless to say, Felt's invention gave the early calculating machine a new dimension in speed. Felt called his commercial keyboard machine a comptometer. He set up a company to market his brainchild, which proved highly successful in the business field.

The honor of adding a numerical keyboard system to a calculating machine was not Felt's alone, however. He shared some of this with another American inventor, William S. Burroughs (1857–1898). In creating his mechanical computer, Burroughs also incorporated a numerical keyboard. In addition, Burroughs gave his adding machine a printing unit that recorded numerical sums on paper.

Like Felt, Burroughs established a company to market his adding machine. The company became hugely successful and with the arrival of the modern electronic era, made the transition to the new breed of electronic computers without difficulty.

Another American inventor who participated in the evolution of the mechanical computer was Herman Hollerith (1860–1929). Hollerith's contribution to the machine's development was twofold. One part related to the technical aspect of the machine and the other to the type of work of which his invention was capable.

Hollerith was inspired by a problem that the federal government faced in processing census data. Up until 1890 counting heads in the nation had been done laboriously by hand by an army of counters. Now with an increasing influx of immigrants from Europe and elsewhere, the nation's population was growing by leaps and bounds.

Counting and sorting data involving millions of people was becoming physically impractical. Years passed before results could be tabulated. In fact, before the task could be completed, ten years would have passed, and it would be time to take another census count.

Hollerith figured out a way to get over the hurdle by using a punch card system with a machine he called a tabulator. His unique system of employing Jacquard's punched cards was considerably more advanced than the card arrangement devised by Babbage. The American inventor's system could process mountains of figures without difficulty.

After Hollerith convinced government officials that his machine was an effective solution to their problem, they agreed to put it to work processing the census count of 1890. The tabulator came through the task with flying colors. The job was completed a good deal faster and more easily than if done by human processors.

In the aftermath of this success, Hollerith soon demonstrated that he was just as astute a businessman as he was an inventor. He established the Tabulating Machine Company in 1896 to build and market his data processing machine. Evidently its effective use in the census of 1890 proved a stimulus for sales. Business was brisk right from the start. Commercial enterprises saw the tabulator as a way of making the paperwork portion of their business more efficient and less costly.

While profits soared, Hollerith shifted his attention from the company's engineering activities to its financial aspect. Alert and aggressive, he began acquiring other business machine companies both in this country and abroad. By continuing to expand through the early decades of this century Hollerith made his company one of the largest for the manufacture of business machines.

After it had swallowed up a number of competitors and had begun to manufacture more than just tabulators, the company changed its name to International Business Machines, or IBM. Today the descendant of Hollerith's enterprise is a giant in the manufacturing of electronic computers and other business equipment.

Many other inventive individuals of course, both in this country and abroad, were involved in the development of mechanical computers and their many variations. What these creative people had achieved by the beginning of the twentieth century, and for a decade or two thereafter, with their diverse mechanical contrivances was quite remarkable.

As the current era dawned, there was scarcely a business concern of any size that did not have one or more mechanical and electromechanical computers, tabulators, and card punch machines to help workers cope with the ever increasing quantities of paperwork more efficiently and at less cost. There is little doubt that had there been no age of electronics, the mechanical world of computers and other business machines would have continued to be technically improved. This is the way of inventors, seeking always to improve that which already exists.

The reign of the mechanical computer continued supreme throughout the early decades of this century. But its days were numbered. The machine's role in the history of technology was to end with the discovery of a tiny atomic particle called the electron.

The electron, a negatively charged atomic particle, had been discovered by the English physicist, Joseph Thompson in 1897. Twenty years later other scientists and technologists had gathered so much knowledge about the particle that it was rapidly becoming the subject of a science all its own. The radio was one of the earliest practical demonstrations of what the electron, when properly controlled, could do.

No one really had any idea of the potential of this tiny particle of matter. But when the science of electronics really started to come into its own under the technological impetus of World War II, the impact of its achievements was nothing short of shattering. As for its effect on mechanical computers, electronics and its newborn twin microelectronics sent these machines off to museums. The metallic clacking of the mechanical calculators gave way to the silent magic of flashing electrons.

The ENIAC—Electronic Numerical Integrator and Calculator—was the world's first practical digital electronic computer. The mammoth room-size machine owed its existence to J. Presper Eckert and John W. Mauchly, scientists of the Moore School of Electrical engineering at the University of Pennsylvania.

The giant ENIAC contained eighteen thousand tubes, which produced so much heat that special air-conditioning equipment was required. The wiring that formed its circuits and connected its components would have stretched several miles if placed end to end. All who were present at ENIAC's unveiling in 1946 were awed not only by its huge size but also by its performance. The computer astounded onlookers by multiplying a five-digit number by itself five thousand times in half a second.

ENIAC's main task was to calculate complex bal-

The ENIAC—Electronic Numerical Integrator and
Calculator—befitting its long, formal name, was a
colossal room-size computer. Completed in 1946, the
huge machine was powered by 18,000 tubes. It could
multiply a five-digit number by itself five thousand times
in half a second. Today, the microchip has reduced these
giant machines to pigmy size.

listic trajectories for the U.S. Army's Ordnance Department, which it did for a number of years.

Modern computers and other electronic equipment have little in common with their nineteenth-century ancestors except for certain basic elements. And even these have been transformed for electronic functioning so that they bear little resemblance to their original counterparts.

Over the past decade, library shelves have been filled with books about the nature and workings of computers. It is not our intention here to add to this avalanche of publications. Those who are interested in the technical details relating to the complex innards of computers should consult the bibiography at the end of this book for some helpful titles.

However, we will pause to see in some detail a few of the computer's principal elements and the role they play in helping the machine perform its wizardry.

Almost forty years ago when electronic computers were in the early stages of development, one of the chief participants in that work, John von Neumann, stated that a typical digital computer carries out its work by employing four basic functions: input, output, processing, and control storage. The more modern computer sometimes varies these by expanding that number to input, memory, arithmetics and logic, control, and finally output.

Input

Before a computer can do any kind of work it must be instructed in what is expected of it. Some kind of communication must exist between the operator and the machine to bring this about. This is achieved by a number of different devices that translate input information, such as data and program instructions, into a code, or language, that the computer understands.

Among the first input devices to be used were punched cards that Babbage and Hollerith employed for their inventions. Now there are numerous others including punched tapes, magnetic tapes, floppy discs, and drums with magnetized surfaces. Some later developments include optical scanners capable of recognizing characters at high speeds and electronic devices called ears that have the ability to pick up and react correctly to a few spoken words. This unit is often referred to as a voice synthesizer.

Another input device with which we are all familiar is the telephone, the touch-tone type. The prediction is that as home computers become more widely used for communicating with a variety of outside data sources, the telephone will be a commonly employed input device. Anticipating this, the makers of the touch-tone telephone have already equipped the instrument with two special buttons. They will permit the user to communicate at the touch of a button with specific data banks and to tap a computer's particular components for processing other information.

In the same category as the telephone is the omnipresent TV set. This, too, promises to be a computer post in the future. In fact, it already is on a small scale, with more and more sets being made with plug-in connections for external units like a keyboard for tapping data into the machine.

The input information comes in a variety of forms. The information may consist of images, letters, numbers, sounds, marks, or magnetized ink on cards, paper, or tape. These are transformed by the appropriate devices in a computer into patterns of electrical pulses that the machine can interpret and then perform accordingly.

Memory

Every computer has a memory unit. Without it the machine would be useless. The memory portion of the computer is the brain and heart of the machine. The memory unit stores specific information along with the programmed instructions for gaining access to the information.

For almost twenty years when all sorts of computers were coming on the market, the most common type of memory device used was the magnetic core. This is a complex arrangement involving a checkerboard pattern of wires and minute magnetized iron rings. There are thousands of these rings in the memory unit.

At the point where the two wires of the checkerboard pattern intersect, forming a cross, there is a ring. There are hundreds of these rings. Every ring stores either a 1 or a 0 in the computer's binary numerical system. The two wires—and there are thousands of these—pass through each doughnut-shaped ring.

An electric current flows through the two ring-encircled wires. The direction in which this current travels determines how each tiny ring is magnetized.

Thus, the magnetic action might be clockwise or counterclockwise.

In the computer's communication code, this magnetic flow is registered as a 1 or 0. This in turn indicates an instantaneous electronic switching action, on or off. The 1 or 0 also represents a "bit," a tiny portion of the data stored in the memory ring. The word derives from *bi*nary *dig*it. This is the numerical arrangement that digital computers use for presenting information.

The magnetic core memory unit is truly a remarkable piece of technology. It can perform not only with great speed but with uncanny accuracy as well. This accuracy is the result of its gridlike pattern. Each minute memory ring is located exactly in the pattern so that it has a predetermined "street" and "avenue" address.

When the computer's code system is activated, the electric current knows precisely what ring to go to to tap the required source of information. All of this can take place in about the time it takes to blink an eye.

One other element must be involved before a ring can release its data. This is a third wire that also passes through the ring's center. Along this electrified metallic avenue the core information travels to the computer's display screen.

In the jargon of computer experts, the type of memory device just described belongs to the group of such units called RAM, or *R*andom *A*ccess *M*emory. This type of memory permits information to be added, deleted, or changed. The principal drawback of RAM is that once power is shut off, the information in the unit disappears.

This does not happen with ROM, or Read Only Memory. This memory device has its information in a permanent form, and it does not vanish when power is cut off. However, the data cannot be added to or altered.

Computers generally have backup or auxiliary memories, too. These secondary units may be in the form of magnetic tapes or floppy discs. They are important because they are capable of holding a large number of data and are a good deal less expensive than a core unit. Computer users who have quantities of information to store generally make use of the auxiliary units. The main and auxiliary memory units can be interconnected for ready access.

It may readily be seen that the magnetic core memory unit just described is an extremely fragile device and therefore costly to make. Despite these traits it has served as a workhorse in the computer world for close to two decades. Today it has largely been replaced by the memory chip, either RAM or ROM.

Still another memory type, and one of growing usefulness, is the magnetic bubble. It was invented in 1967 at Bell Labs, source of countless microelectronic creations. The magnetic bubble memory gets its name from thousands of tiny microscopic bumps or bubbles that are formed and magnetized in a thin film of magnetized material. The bubbles become highly mobile when a magnetic field is applied. They move, under control, along precise lines of travel. As the bubbles move swiftly along the magnetic tracks, they pass stationary magnetized points. These points record the presence of a bubble, or its absence. The action is read as coded information.

A typical logic microchip. This is a greatly enlarged photo of a device only ¼ of an inch square.

Courtesy IBM Corporation

The memory chip, a vital part in all modern computers, can hold an incredible amount of information. A standard type currently in use holds 64,000 bits of data. IBM has developed an experimental version that is capable of storing 524,000 bits of data. This superb technical achievement prefigures a new breed of computers within the next few years with even more magical abilities than these machines now possess. As an example of the amount of information a memory chip of this advanced variety can hold, it is said that the contents of the Encyclopedia Britannica could be put on the chip with room to spare.

Central Processing Unit (CPU)

Any computer, whether mechanical or electronic, must be able to handle or process the flow of input data in accordance with the computer's programmed instructions. This is accomplished by another of the computer's critical parts—the Central Processing Unit, or CPU. This element, also referred to as a microprocessor, consists of three principal components: the logic unit, the arithmetic unit, and a control unit. The CPU enables the computer to carry out what it performs best, crunching numbers in a spectacular fashion.

The control portion of the CPU has been called the computer's traffic officer. It takes the instructions that are stored in the memory unit, interprets them, and acts accordingly.

Chief among these actions is the regulation of the memory, arithmetic, and logic components so they do exactly what is expected of them. Part of this task of the control unit involves regulating the movement of information among the memory, arithmetic, and logic units.

Finally, it is the CPU's task to direct the processed data from the memory unit along the required circuits to the output section of the computer.

Output

After digesting the input instructions and the related stored data, the computer presents the finished product to the operator. This may be done in several different ways.

The output unit may transform the finished data into electrical impulses that in turn operate a number of readout devices. The readout devices can present the results as words or numbers on the face of a cathode ray tube (CRT), which looks much like a TV screen.

In some computers the readout is presented by voice synthesizer devices on floppy discs, punched cards, or magnetic tape. Usually the readout information is made use of directly by the computer operator. In other instances, however, the finished data may end up in written form exiting from another computer miles away.

When computers relay information to one another, the readout data may travel along a tele-communications network, or the coded signals may be beamed over ultra-high-frequency airways. A truly astonishing demonstration of such a hookup occurs when computers at control stations on the earth communicate with computers aboard unmanned spacecraft speeding millions of miles away through the cosmos.

Computers are basically mathematical machines that do their work by means of a numerical code. Two principal types are employed, the digital computer and the analog computer. Both operate at incredible speed.

As its name indicates, the digital computer does its work solely by numbers. It uses the binary system consisting of 1 and 0. In the computer's electronic circuitry 1 and 0 are comparable to on and off switches. When the 1 initiates an electrical impulse, one of the computer's many internal switches is on, the 0 activates an electrical impulse that closes a similar switch. This switching job is the responsibility of one or more transistors incorporated into the microchip.

In a sense, the binary number system is a computer code that can be juggled to produce any numerical quantity. These quantities in turn are translated into electrical pulses that may be transformed back into a computer's language. As we have also noted, the results may be in the form of words on the screen of a cathode ray tube or as words printed on paper, so-called hard copy.

Another feature of the binary system is the identification it makes with a computer's capabilities. For example, a computer that has a 32 K RAM device or a 128 K RAM device has a memory chip that contains 32,000 or 128,000 bits of data.

As a measure of a computer's memory storage capacity and power, the bit has been given a specific value, 1024. This sum of bits is referred to as a kilobit, or K-1024 bits. Kilo (K) in the metric system of measurement represents one thousand.

Knowing the value of K it is a simple matter to determine that a computer with 32 K RAM power has a memory chip with a capacity of 32,768 bits of information ($32 \times 1024 = 32,768$). Letters and numbers are represented by a number of bits in combination. The unit is called a byte. There are eight bits to a byte.

The second computer type is called the analog computer. It, too, can calculate but in quite a different way from the digital machine. Basically it operates by measuring continuously a physical quantity like an electrical current or a voltage output.

The quantity or quantities being measured by the computer are analogous, or similar, to the quantities being fed into the machine. This nondigital computer has particular application for controlling processes that are continuous in nature as in oil refining or a chemical production line.

To make particular use of a computer's binary code system the user must prepare a program and feed it into the machine. This program or set of instructions really tells the machine what the user wants it to do. It is known as computer software. A computer does not begin to operate on any kind of processing work simply by having its keyboard punched. It must be programmed or instructed what to do, and this is the assignment of software.

In a number of instances special computer languages have been created where the computer's use is restricted to a particular field of work. FORTRAN was an early computer language designed to instruct a computer to do a wide variety of technical and scientific research applications. FORTRAN is an acronym derived from *FOR*mula *TRAN*slation. COBOL, from *CO*mmon *B*usiness *O*riented *L*anguage, is another specialized computer language. It is used for a large array of business office activities. Others in a growing list of computer languages are BASIC and APC. Creating languages for computer programs is a difficult assignment.

The program flexibility that is so characteristic of modern computers did not always exist. Back in the early years of electronic computers, at the time of ENIAC in the mid-1940s, programming these giants was a far different story.

Once one of these behemoths had been programmed to carry out a specific set of instructions, it was terribly difficult to change the program or to give the machine a new one. Changing a program at that time meant tearing a computer almost completely apart and putting it back together again. To do this on a room-size machine, with thousands of wires to be disconnected and connected, was an enormously tedious and costly operation. A brilliant Hungarian physicist and mathematician, John von Neumann, conceived an idea that would overcome this computer deficiency.

Neumann had seen ENIAC when the monster machine first began operating. He was greatly impressed by its calculating abilities. While pleased with their machine's phenomenal calculating performance, the creators disclosed to Neumann ENIAC's shortcoming with respect to programming. They realized this problem would have to be overcome if the giant computer was ever to realize its fullest potential.

Neumann's keen mind considered the problem and before long came up with an ingenious solution. He proposed that the data to be processed and instructions for carrying out this part of the computer's performance be put into the same memory unit. Further, he suggested that the same code be employed for doing both jobs.

The builders of ENIAC received the mathematician's concept enthusiastically. Shortly after hearing Neumann's proposal, they decided to incorporate a memory storage unit of that type in their more advanced computer, the EDVAC.

In its ultimate development, John von Neumann's idea meant that the computer would have the ability to change programs easily and swiftly with its processing unit. Properly programmed machines would also have the added feature of deciding when to make such changes.

When carried to its ultimate development, Neumann's computer concept made it possible for one program to change another program and even to change itself as the need arose. It remained for the mighty microchip, the size of a child's fingernail, to bring into practical use von Neumann's tremendously significant computer idea.

Christopher Evans in his masterful account of the development of the computer put the importance of Neumann's contribution this way: "In one conceptual jump, the true power of computers moved from the finite to the potentially infinite."

In the following pages we shall see some of the varied examples of the computer's finite and potentially infinite power.

4

The Versatile Chip

The first electronic computers that appeared in the late 1940s and 1950s were giant machines that occupied an entire room. They were enormously expensive to build and highly specialized in the kind of work they could perform (mainly calculations), and they required well-trained operators. There were not many in existence during that period. In fact, aside from ENIAC there was only one other. In the 1960s, newer models appeared, and these were immediately employed by the federal government, large business corporations, and scientific research organizations.

The federal government was the first to employ these huge number-crunchers. They were put to work counting and analyzing the census results of 1950. They proved extremely effective in speeding up this gigantic job. As a result, the government ordered several additional models. When these became operational, they were assigned such varied tasks as working out the ballistic trajectories of intercontinental missiles for the Defense Department; helping to design nuclear reactors; deciphering and creating intelligence codes; and keeping track of the government's vast inventory of property.

By the time the 1960s came to an end, the computer picture was changing swiftly and drastically. The microchip had been born and was revolutionizing the structure and operating abilities of computers. The size of computers was shrinking rapidly, from giant stature to midget. Indeed, some were so small they could be carried in a coat pocket.

With the dramatic change in size came an equally startling transformation in the uses to which computers were put. They were no longer used solely to solve mathematical problems. Now they were given diverse jobs ranging from controlling a microwave oven in the family kitchen to guiding a spacecraft through the cosmos. The computer had acquired an electronic brain.

Another notable development in the transformation of the computer resulted from the employment of the microchip: the rapid growth of computer users. When the giant machines were the only types in existence, not many people were involved with their operation. Today, computer users are in the millions, and their number is still expanding.

The electronic revolution, which many compare to the Industrial Revolution of the sixteenth, seventeenth, and eighteenth centuries, in a little more than two decades has had nearly as significant an impact on modern society. It has created technological upheavals, and it is bringing about drastic changes in the way we live. And the flood tide of change that this present-day technological revolution has set in motion is still running at full strength with scarcely a sign of letting up.

The infinite potential of the computer, the focal object of the electronic revolution, has begun to manifest itself in a number of impressive ways indeed. What follows is a general survey of some of the innovations that the chip and the computer are bringing about.

Computers and the Business World

The early mechanical computers were created solely to help with business tasks. They performed calculations, rendered bills, kept track of inventories, along with other chores. As the machines improved technically, the range of uses to which they were put also increased. This close association between the computer, more popularly called a calculator then, and the business world continued after the dawn of the electronic era. Today, the alliance between the two is closer than ever. Indeed, the modern business world could hardly be managed without the aid of computers and other microelectronic equipment and services. Every facet of business—from routine tasks like billing and filing to management duties involving analysis and decision-making—is in some measure aided or influenced by the computer.

Information is vital for the successful operation of business. The conventional data banks are the filing cabinets. Information may also be stored in a secretary's head, in desk drawers, or on appointment calendars. Usually when information is needed, it is wanted in a hurry. Speed is not always possible with the manual or paper system. Now a far more efficient and faster method is made possible by the microchip, which is used in an array of microelectronics equipment. And, to management's delight, this new method is a good deal less costly than the older arrangement.

The electronic system for storing information is known as electronic filing. This involves a variety of equipment that stores information in a digital form within some kind of electronic storage-access unit. One such popular type of storage unit is a magnetic disc that looks much like a long-playing record.

The information on a magnetic disc is generally retrieved by tapping the keys of a computer's keyboard. The desired information shows up on the machine's viewing screen.

More sophisticated filing and retrieval systems may employ electronic devices for handling facsimile, photographic, micrographic, and TV signals.

One of the really startling new electronic business office aids is the word processor. The machine is essentially a computer that deals with words rather than with numbers. It is especially valuable to typists and writers preparing letters and documents from company data. In fact, this type of computer is extremely helpful to all those who work with words, such as authors of articles and books.

Word processors like the one shown are a great boon in many offices.

Courtesy Dictaphone

The word processor, as we said, is essentially a computer with a keyboard similar to that of a typewriter for putting information into the machine. It also has a CRT (cathode ray tube) screen for terminal display of material and a printer device that turns out finished hard copy on paper. The machine contains other units found in the conventional computer: a memory device, usually a RAM (random access memory), and the heart of the machine, the central processing unit (CPU), with its magic chip.

A tremendously versatile performer, the word processor permits the user to delete, add, or transpose words and whole paragraphs from one place to another in the copy being worked on. If the user wants to insert new material on a particular page, he or she simply punches the proper key, and the processor, with uncanny accuracy, automatically finds the correct page and place for the insertion.

By punching other keys, the user can direct the word processor to store the new information in its memory bank. Finally, the user can command the processor to renumber the pages if insertion makes that necessary. All this can be done while the remainder of the text is left undisturbed.

One component of the word processor that is helpful to many users is its dictionary bank. The processor can store words, correctly spelled and hyphenated, on magnetic tape or disc. The processor's dictionary bank may contain several thousand words that are used frequently. It also has room for additional words or phrases that are commonly used in the particular field in which the operator of the word processor is working—scientific research, engineering, or law, for example. Word processors can automatically spot misspelled words and so inform the operator.

The biggest asset of a word and data processing system is speed. It can reduce the time needed to do a special job assignment from days to hours.

Other electronic office helpers include electronic mail systems and copiers that reproduce printed material. The mail system delivers messages via a computerized hookup between two or more points of business operations. The system might also involve such transmission methods as sound, a computerized-text communications arrangement, or a graphics display terminal. The electronic mail system is becoming increasingly popular because of its speed and because it drastically reduces the amount of paperwork that can overwhelm office operations. With Uncle Sam constantly raising the cost of hand-delivered mail service, the electronic mail system is becoming increasingly more attractive to businesses seeking to reduce the costs of operations.

To meet mail delivery competition and to speed up its mail service, the U.S. Postal Service, which is a very large business enterprise, has developed and put into operation an electronic mail system of its own. The Postal Service has long been criticized for the snail's pace at which it moves mail around the country.

E-COM (Electronic Computer Originated Mail), the Postal Service's system, is a two-day computerized service. Subscribers to it pay an annual fee and prepare their messages on computers. These are then sent via the telephone or other telecommunications systems to designated receiving stations scattered throughout the country.

The messages at the receiving stations are converted into printed form, placed in special envelopes, and then delivered to their destinations as conventional mail.

E-COM began operating in January 1982, and it was well received by many business firms. For one thing it relieved them of the burden of setting up an electronic mail system of their own. In many cases a saving was also involved because the Postal Service provided the paper, envelopes, and postage.

Present-day business offices and their methods of operation are light years ahead of those that were in existence fifty years ago. Banks, insurance firms, utilities, and corporations with global interests have been especially active in transforming their offices into centers of sophisticated electronic operations. As computers and other electronic equipment for office use become more versatile, the number of employees needed to do the work is gradually being reduced. Those who remain are rapidly becoming highly trained monitors and supervisors of electronic automatons.

The Military and Microelectronics

The military establishment in this country has long been closely related to electronics. The military, as we have seen, provided a large measure of support during the early years for research and development in microelectronics. In fact, it was mainly because of the support of the U.S. military forces that transistors, microchips, and computers advanced to the level of sophistication at which they now stand.

The impact that microelectronics has had on the military has been just as great as the impact on the rest of American society. War weapons for air, land, and sea have been radically transformed from what they were a quarter of a century ago. Much of the burden of operating the weapons has shifted from the fighting men to the microchip. Highly sophisticated as they are, current weapons are considered only a prelude to even more exotic tools of war similar to those that science-fiction writers have been describing for years.

Modern military aircraft are almost totally dependent on microelectronic devices and equipment for carrying out their exacting assignments. Fighter planes, for example, that engage in individual combat are a far cry from those of the Red Baron era of World War I. Aircraft then were little more than manned powered kites of wood, canvas, and baling wire. In those days the pilot made the plane respond to his wishes.

This is not true of the thundering, bullet-fast supersonic jet fighter planes that streak through the skies. Modern aircraft are packed with electronic gear, mainly small, fast-operating digital computers. These devices help the pilot fly his swift aerial vehicle through all sorts of twisting maneuvers and also keep him continuously informed about the opponent he is pursuing.

Modern fighter jet planes are not only fast but also very heavy. Many weigh more than 8 tons, so that pilots really need electromechanical aids to manage them, particularly during aerial combat. Because of the plane's swiftness, decision-making has to be almost instantaneous. This is where the minicomputers aboard the aircraft are proving indispensable. To dive, climb, or perform a looping, turning maneuver, a jet pilot need only press lightly on a control stick button that instantly activates the appropriate computer. Responding instantly to the command, the computer flashes an electrical signal that moves the plane's tail and wings, causing it to execute the desired maneuver.

Still other computers aboard the lightning-swift fighter plane are linked to a small radar unit that keeps the fighter pilot constantly informed about the plane he is pursuing. The other plane's speed, direction, and altitude are displayed on a small glass panel between the pilot and the windshield. This is the readout of the radar-computer system called Head-Up Display (HUD). This eliminates the need for a pilot to focus his eyes downward on the instrument panel and away from the vitally important forward line of sight.

At the pilot's fingertips there are also button controls that electronically fire the plane's missiles at the precise moment of attack, that automatically feed more fuel to the aircraft's powerful jet engines to increase speed, and that perform a variety of other operations. The air-to-air missiles may have tiny radar-computer devices of their own that unerringly guide the weapon to a target. Others are equipped with heat-seeking units that find the exhaust of an enemy's jet engine and send the destructive missile directly into it.

Versatile computerized systems aboard modern fighter planes have relieved pilots of almost all manual control. Once instructed by the human pilots, computers literally take over guidance of the aircraft. It has been said that the human pilot has now become little more than an observer, although he still calls the signals for the needed battle tactics.

A new kind of military aircraft has come into existence as a direct result of a microelectronic development known as computer and airborne radar. This plane is called AWACS (Airborne Warning and Control System). It is a standard commercial aircraft converted for its military role by radar, computers, and a large array of other complex microelectronic equipment. Its chief purpose is to detect invading aircraft and then cruise about like a

This cutaway view of an AWACS plane shows the variety of its electronic equipment.

Courtesy Boeing Aircraft Corporation

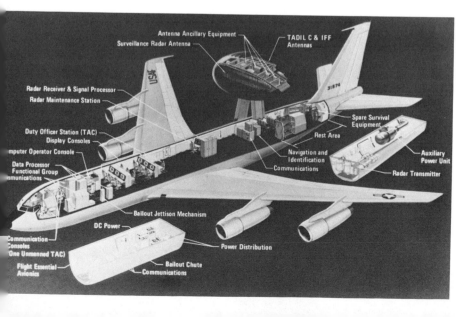

command post in the sky to help the defending aircraft ward off the attackers. This role is the reason the aircraft is sometimes called the "battle management" plane.

The AWACS aircraft provides electronic help not only by detecting unfriendly planes but also by tracking their movements. It tracks other aircraft by sweeping the sky with its radar eye, which can encompass more than two hundred planes. With the additional help of an array of computers, the AWACS crew can quickly provide the pilots of defending planes with more than a dozen solutions for intercepting a similar number of unfriendly aircraft. The information is flashed instantly over a compatible communications system.

The uncanny intelligence of the microelectronics equipment aboard the AWACS plane is so refined that it can even tell friend from foe during the course of battle. The AWACS demonstrated its sophisticated capabilities in the Middle East war of 1982 between the Israelis and the Syrians. A battle management plane helped Israeli pilots shoot down over thirty Syrian aircraft without a single loss of their own.

Other computer-controlled equipment and instruments have made flying military aircraft safer and a good deal easier than it used to be. Since much of this electronic apparatus has been adapted for commercial planes as well, their flight safety and ease of operation have also been greatly enhanced. The electronic brain, shrunken by the magic chip in size to fit the restricted space of the modern plane, monitors a host of aircraft functions like oil pressure, fuel consumption, and sudden emergency conditions. In addition, a special electronic brain unit in the form of an automatic pilot can fly an aircraft completely on its own. This is a special advantage for the flight crew since it gives them a chance to rest from their duties while traveling a long-distance air route.

The newer electronic equipment can navigate as well as direct the flight of an aircraft. Here again the computer plays a large role in accomplishing the job. Employing the additional assistance of the navigational space satellite NAVSTAR, flight crews aboard a plane can find their position over any point on earth in a matter of minutes, to within 30 feet.

Another piece of military equipment that has been improved by microelectronics is the ponderous battle tank which has been transformed into an even more destructive war machine than it was before. Minicomputers linked to radar systems now allow a tank crew to ferret out an enemy at night and in bad weather with greatly improved accuracy. The tank's computer-controlled guns have also been made far more deadly.

Cruise missiles—pilotless aircraft—and "smart bombs" are unerringly guided to targets by specially programmed minicomputers or by extremely sensitive on-board electronic receivers that respond to external instructions. If an enemy position far behind a battle zone is the objective to be attacked, the enemy would unquestionably try to shoot it down as it passed over his territory. To cope with that situation, the missile's electronic brain will activate a new set of instructions that enable the aerial weapon to take evasive action.

This country's military forces were among the first to put supercomputers to work. These computers still play a key role in the nation's defense. At vital air defense centers, for example, batteries of electronic math wizards stand ready to track and intercept attacking nuclear armed intercontinental missiles. Others are employed at military headquarters to work out problems associated with planning and strategy. Supercomputers are also demonstrating their great value in weapons research, as well as helping the military keep accurate personnel records.

Along with the drastic changes taking place in weapons as a result of the development of electronics, a radical transformation of the soldier is also occurring. He is no longer being trained solely in elementary military activities but is also learning to operate highly complicated machinery of war.

The Medical World and Microelectronics

Modern medicine has made giant strides in combating the diverse ills that afflict humanity. Among the first important weapons to be developed in this century to fight illness have been the so-called miracle or wonder drugs. Now, with the dawn of microelectronics and the wizardry of the microchip, newer equipment and techniques have come into existence that have enormously strengthened the efforts of the medical profession.

The electronic medical aids range from simple fingernail-size devices to complex machines. They perform in such areas of the medical field as diagnosis, the treatment of certain ailments, and the creation of sophisticated prosthetic devices. In addition, microelectronics is also helping in the business areas and the physical activities of running a hospital or large medical center.

The specific medical services of microelectronics are many and diverse. One of the earliest medical electronic helpers to appear was the tiny heart pacemaker. Small enough to be implanted in a patient's chest, the pacemaker monitors heart rhythms. The newer types now available have been improved so that they monitor and correct a number of different kinds of irregular heart rhythms. In fact, this minicomputerlike device is so versatile that doctors believe its potential for helping heart patients has not been fully exhausted.

The defibrillator is another electronic medical aid for people with more serious heart rhythm problems. Out of the development stage only a short while, this computerized device can also be implanted in a patient's body. It detects potentially serious irregularities in the heartbeat and then automatically, by means of an electrical shock of the correct intensity, restores the heart to its normal rhythm.

Serious heart rhythm problems are responsible for hundreds of deaths annually. Now, thanks to this microelectronic device, many victims may have a new lease on life.

One of the major contributions of microelectronics to the medical field is the CAT—Computerized Axial Tomography—scan. This X-ray machine is capable of detecting the differences between internal body tissue with fifty times greater effectiveness than ordinary X-ray machines.

The key to the CAT scanner's superior operation is the computerization of the findings of the machine's scanning element. The findings are synthesized into diagnostic data, which the doctor interprets. The CAT scan has become a powerful aid for detecting the presence of tumors and other diseased tissue within the body.

Medical scientists have long known that X-rays can be harmful as well as beneficial. Prolonged exposure to these powerful rays can damage healthy body tissue while destroying diseased tissue. Now this danger may soon be a thing of the past with new X-ray equipment and handling techniques resulting from the application of microelectronics technology.

The new type machine has a unit called a scintillator fixed to a movable arm above the patient lying on a table. As X-rays are directed at the patient's body, the scintillator picks them up, converts them into electrical impulses, and sends them to a computer that changes them into a picture on the terminal screen.

The creators of this new X-ray equipment estimate that patients exposed to its beams receive less than 1 percent of the harmful radiation they would get from conventional X-ray machines. Improved versions of the computerized X-ray equipment are expected to reduce radiation danger even more in the future.

Another area of medicine to which microelectronics has made a startling contribution is in

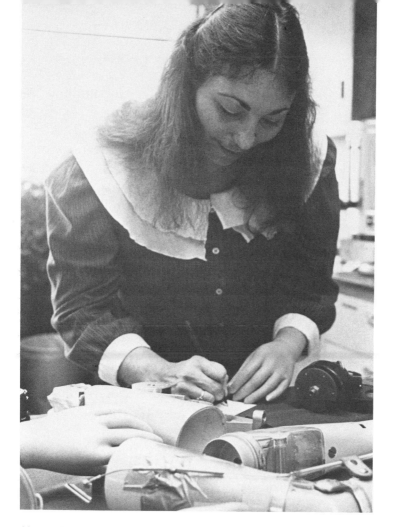

Microelectronics are playing an increasing role in helping amputees. This woman has been fitted with a newly developed, totally electric "elbow" and hand system.

Courtesy University of Utah Public Relations

prosthetics—the replacement of parts of the human body that have been damaged by deformities, illness, or injuries. These replaced parts are called prostheses.

With the help of microelectronics technology, astonishing prostheses have been created. Many of these have been the work of scientists and technicians at university and medical research centers. Some of the most unusual achievements have made it possible for doctors to replace or reactivate damaged nerve tissue. Victims of paralysis, for example, are being helped by the magic of microelectronics which replaces or restores muscle power. For amputees, mechanical arms and legs of uncanny mobility are becoming increasingly available through the use of tiny electric motors controlled by minicomputers.

Computer-controlled electric shock also can restore movement to paralyzed arms and legs. For instance, computerized electronic equipment was strapped to the legs of one young paraplegic. With the application of electric current, the patient was able to walk a few steps.

Deaf people were the first to experience the valuable contribution of microelectronics. The miniature hearing aid brought help to many. Now they stand to benefit even further from the development of tiny devices capable of turning sound waves into electronic impulses and sending them to the auditory nerve that controls hearing.

Through the magic of microelectronics, scientists are also making progress toward giving the blind a measure of sight. A successful demonstration was given of a tiny plastic device containing electrodes implanted in the part of the brain that controls sight. Wires from the device were linked to a computer. They served as an electrical path for a flow of current to the brain. When the sight-controlling portion of the brain was stimulated in this way, a blind test patient was able to see pinpoints of light.

This research and development work is only in the early stages. But the scientists and technicians involved feel that eventually they will succeed to the point where they can make a significant difference in the lives of people who have lost their sight.

The medical profession has fought humanity's ills for decades with drugs and surgery. Microelectronics has given the profession a new and powerful reinforcement that should become even more important in the future.

Industry and Microelectronics

Industry discovered early that microelectronics offered enormous benefits in the way of speeding the production of goods and cutting costs. Many tasks in the manufacturing and processing fields that were once done by human workers are now being performed by electromechanical automatons, or robots.

The use of robots instead of people to do useful work is not new. Back in the 1950s industrial engineers were designing and building elementary robots to perform repetitive manufacturing jobs such as drilling and tapping holes. Then as now, the principal reason for using them was to cut manufacturing costs.

The word "robot," commonly used in today's automated factory, had its origin back in 1923 when it was first used in the play *R.U.R.* (Rossum's Universal

Robots) by Karel Čapek (1890–1938), a Czechoslovakian playwright. This science-fiction play depicted a future society in which robots did all the physical labor in the factories and on the farms. Čapek's play ends in disaster when the robots revolt and kill their human masters. *R.U.R.* is rarely performed today, but the word "robot" endured and has become entrenched in our language.

Karel Čapek's fictional robots were created chemically. Today's robots, of course, are electromechanical creatures with computers for brains. They exist in all sizes, large and small, and in a variety of forms. When at work they generally remain in a fixed location, although they can be moved to other work stations in a factory if necessary.

Industries whose products require a large number of manufacturing steps, such as the automobile and aerospace fields, have found robots particularly valuable in making their production lines more efficient. With metallic grippers for hands, movable mechanical arms, and computer brains, these artificial workers can tighten bolts, drill holes, make spot welds, and paint parts hour after hour. They stop only when their programmed instructions tell them to or when the electric power in the factory is shut off.

Not all human factory workers like robots, as we shall soon see. But these man-made creatures do have friends; among them are workers who are assigned dirty, hot, unpleasant jobs such as welding or painting. More and more robots are taking over these tasks and working without complaint, or coffee breaks, for as long as they are directed to.

This master computer control station continually monitors fifty-eight robots on a welding line at a Chrysler auto plant. The plant has sixty-seven other robots that do such jobs as brazing, painting, installing seals around glass windows, and transferring assemblies.

Courtesy Chrysler Corporation

The first industrial robots were "dumb." They could not recognize faults in the work they were doing. For example, if a robot drilled a hole the wrong size or in the wrong place, only the human monitor of the robot could spot the mistake, stop the operation, and correct the problem.

A new breed of robot, with intelligence, is now coming into existence with the promise of being a far superior worker. As robotics technology advances, employing new and improved electronic components, these superior automatons will "see" and have tactile, or feeling, ability. The addition of such sophisticated sensory devices will enable robots to perform more complicated jobs. They will know when a particular operation is not going the way it should and will be able to stop it. Eventually the "brainy" robot is expected to be able to take corrective steps to allow a stopped production line to resume work.

Robotics engineers believe that in some instances, these artificial workers will be able to reduce production costs by as much as 50 percent. One such robot is being employed in an aerospace factory. This computer-controlled worker places thousands of rivets in aircraft structural parts speedily with precision and at a great saving.

The process of converting the human-operated factory to an automated workplace involves devices other than robots, however. Computers by themselves, not linked to another machine or device, are playing important roles. One such electronic industrial aid is called CAD—Computer-Aided Design.

A computerized scanning device checks on the design features of a new model Chrysler vehicle. The resulting information is passed on to a computer-aided-design center for use in actual design, manufacturing engineering, and production.

Courtesy Chrysler Corporation

Before any part or product can be made it must be designed and analyzed. Will it work? Is it the most economical design? The answers to questions like these can easily and quickly be determined by "drawing" the design on the computer's display screen with a light-equipped stylus. In graphic form on the screen, the design can be viewed in three dimensions; it can be rotated around any axis, cross sections can be displayed, and desired changes can be quickly incorporated. The designer can even see how one part will fit in with other parts in an assembly.

Automotive engineers use
computer-aided design (CAD) to create body designs for new cars.
Courtesy Chrysler Corporation

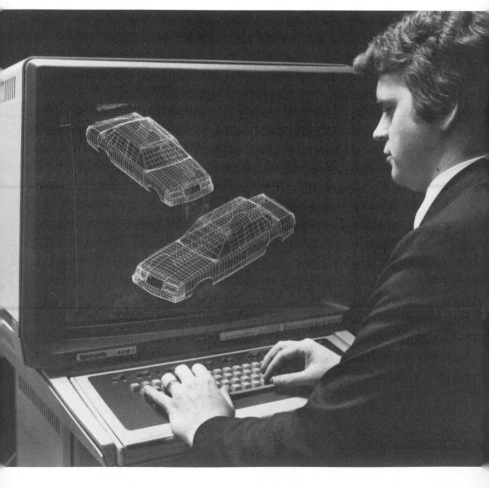

The final design and all the pertinent facts about it can be stored on the computer's memory chip. This information may be recalled at will or transmitted over a telecommunications system to another company division if necessary. The design may also be converted to hard paper copy for distribution to the appropriate personnel in charge of a company's production line.

Speed and great flexibility are the two major characteristics of this type of computer industrial assistance. It has put the slower, more conventional engineering draftsman almost out of business. Companies that have adopted computer-aided design sing its praises. One of the largest auto manufacturers in this country uses CAD to reduce the time needed to make its yearly changeover to new car models. The time required to do this has been reduced from two years to slightly more than a year. Others using this computer design system report similar tremendous savings in time to get a new product on the manufacturing line.

All of these industrial microelectronic aids are major elements in the evolution of a new concept of factory design and operation. The single word dominating this transformation is "automation." Today's factories use a maximum of computer-controlled machines and equipment and a minimum of human workers for production purposes.

As we have already mentioned, one major characteristic of the automated factory is its great flexibility. Modern workplaces allow a manufacturer to reprogram machines quickly and easily for a new product line, or to increase and decrease overall

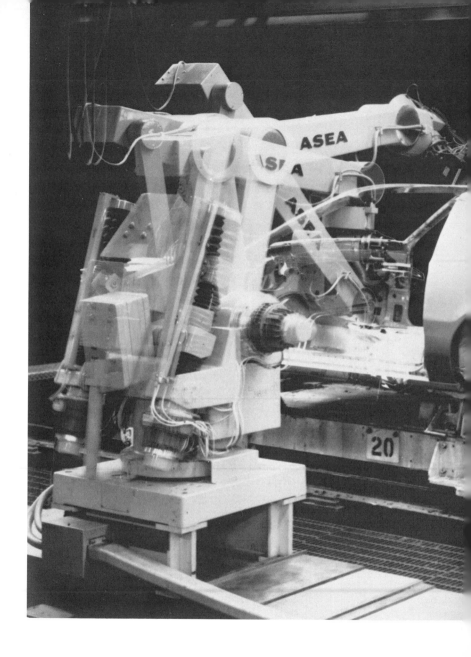

These robots are equipped with optical laser scanners
that permit them to check the dimensions of openings in
car bodies as the cars move along the assembly line.

Courtesy GM Corporation

production as the marketplace dictates. These production capabilities give manufacturers better control of their profit margin.

Automated factories are not futuristic daydreams. They already exist in growing numbers both in the United States, where their major elements were pioneered, and in Japan. It is in the Land of the Rising Sun, however, that the automated factory, with robots and computer-controlled machines and equipment, has been carried to its most advanced level. The Japanese have become world leaders in building and using industrial robots. More than 36,000 automatons are said to be in use in that country as compared with about 15,000 in the United States. Japanese industrialists are enthusiastically plunging ahead, employing more and more man-made workers. Along with computer-aided machines and equipment, they are creating the most highly automated factories in the world.

A fascinating automated workplace is operated by Yamazaki Machinery Works, Ltd., in Japan. The plant is a futurist's dream come true. Within its walls are a large array of computer-run machines and robots, enough to form three football teams. All of these are connected to the company's headquarters twenty miles away by the most up-to-date communications system available.

Like the command post of a military operation, company personnel at the distant headquarters can monitor the computers and instruct them to make certain parts and to use certain tools. The process involves putting into the computer's memory chips the names of the different machine tools needed for the models scheduled for manufacturing. After several buttons have been pushed, the automated factory goes into action. Yamazaki managers proudly claim that their "production plant of the twenty-first century" is the world's first automated workplace to be run by telephone from corporate headquarters. Among this factory's individual automated features is an electronic camera that checks the quality of a finished product. The camera has an electronically operated lens and a magic chip data storage bank. The storage bank contains a detailed description of the perfect product. If the camera's electronic eye spots a finished product with defects—one that does not measure up to the features listed in the data bank—it is removed from the production line.

The Yamazaki robots check production output and load finished items on automatic carriers for transfer to the shipping department. Perhaps the most outstanding feature of this automated plant is that very few human workers are needed to keep it running—only about 250. Their duties are primarily to monitor the man-made workers and make adjustments when needed.

We mentioned earlier that not all human workers look with favor on the invasion of their ranks by robots. It is easy to understand why they feel this way: their own jobs are threatened by the man-made creatures. Unfortunately, this loss of jobs is one of the negative consequences resulting from automated factories.

At this time the social implications of the revolutionary technological development in work are still not too serious. It has been estimated that out of this nation's over 20 million factory workers, only about 20,000 so far have lost their jobs to robots.

According to those who are optimistic about automation, the situation may not become as bad as some foresee. The optimists feel that in the long run, automation will actually create more jobs than it will eliminate. Making robots, servicing them, and monitoring their activities in an automated factory will provide jobs for many human workers.

The pessimists, however, see the changeover from human-run factories to automated workplaces as a potential source of major labor and social crises in the future. To reduce the possibility of such undesirable developments, they are urging that government, labor, management, and social agencies get together to make an exhaustive study of the problem. They feel that the recommendations resulting from such a study could prevent severe economic and social problems. It is already being suggested that one way of dealing with the problem is to retrain workers who have lost their jobs because of automation. The retraining would give them new skills in a high-technology field.

Telecommunications and Microelectronics

The microelectronics revolution, which is currently at full tide, has left its imprint on many human activities, as we have seen. But perhaps the field that has received the greatest technological impact is communications. Indeed, this change has been so

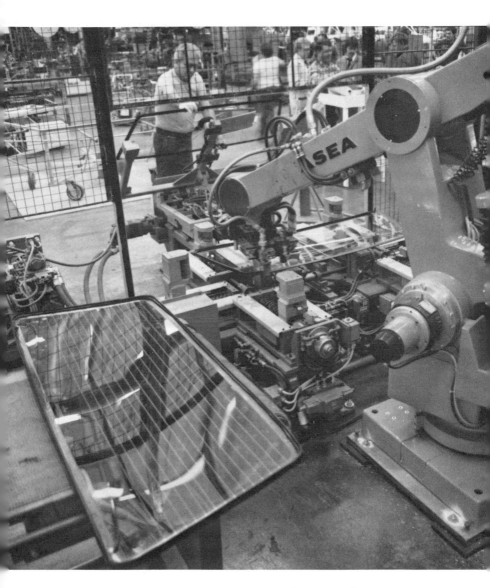

This robot at a Chrysler auto plant is applying a sealer to rear windows before they are installed on vehicles. Another robot does a similar job on windshields.

Courtesy Chrysler Corporation

far-reaching that the word "communications" is being displaced increasingly by a newer term— "telecommunications."

Many in the communications field consider telecommunications a more descriptive word because of the numerous transmission innovations that have come into existence during the current age of microelectronics. Notable among these technical developments has been the role of the versatile computer.

With the proper sending and receiving linkage, computers can exchange data with other computers at any location, nearby or miles away. The binary information sent by a computer can be transformed into electronic pulses that travel via telephone lines to a receiving computer. Arriving at a destination, the signals are changed back into digital form, translated by the computer, and then produced as hard copy or displayed on the terminal screen.

This kind of computer communications network has found favor with many large industrial and commerical corporations that have plants and offices scattered throughout the country. Speed and economy are the system's greatest advantages.

Teleconference communications is another new means of exchanging information. Born of the current microelectronics age, this method of communicating is useful to people who work for the same company but who may be scattered about the country in branch offices. At a designated time the employees at each location gather in teleconference rooms that have large TV screens, computers, and related electronic equipment that allows them to hear and see one another. They can use the TV screens to present company products, charts, and graphics and to talk with one another. Conversations can also be carried on between all the groups. Any individual can get into the discussion simply by pressing appropriate buttons.

More and more corporations are finding the teleconference technique a great convenience. It saves time and eliminates costly travel associated with the conventional method of calling people together at a central location.

The teleconference system is also being adapted by the medical and educational fields. Doctors in different sections of the country are employing the technique to diagnose, discuss, and even treat patients with unusual illnesses.

The system is also useful in the field of education. For instance, a teleconference system connects the University of Wisconsin to scores of libraries, town halls, and other public buildings. Students who cannot attend the university can take courses electronically at one of the receiving stations. Both ends of this telecommunications hookup are equipped with TV, audio, and computer elements. Thus, instructors and students are visible to one another and may carry on a discussion. This telecommunications system has an enormous potential for bringing knowledge and new opportunities to the young and old living in isolated parts of the country.

These telecommunications systems and many others that are currently available rely on the telephone network that laces the nation. This network has been developed over the course of many decades into a marvel of technology. The technical requirements of the fast-growing telephone system created and spurred the development of the tiny transistor. And as we have seen, the transistor started the long and seemingly endless parade of amazing microelectronic devices such as the magic chip. These technical achievements have had no less an impact on the telephone system in this country than on other areas of our modern society.

After evolving for close to a hundred years, the communications system now permits a person to lift the telephone receiver and call another individual anyplace in the nation speedily and automatically. A good portion of the rest of the world is also rapidly being made accessible in the same way in a global communications network. These developments have come to pass largely through the wizardry of microelectronics.

It is estimated that close to a billion telephone calls are made in the United States daily. Handling this immense number of calls swiftly, automatically, and dependably requires a telecommunications system that has been called the largest and most complex mechanism on earth.

On top of the normal demands on the telephone system, there are others—TV transmission, data communications, teletype, and facsimile signals. Thus, it isn't difficult to understand how complex and versatile the telephone network is. Modern technical devices and equipment have given the telephone system the ability to do its enormous job. High-speed digital forms of transmission are linked to automatic electronic switching equipment. These in turn are connected to and controlled by batteries of digital computers, the "brains" of the network.

Computers have given the telephone system a new dimension of intelligence. They handle complicated chores with ease, like the operations related to automatic switching systems. The computers can also spot the nature and location of technical difficulties that arise. To overcome technical problems in the communications network, the computers have the ability to activate backup equipment.

Reliability is one of the chief characteristics of this country's telecommunications network. The large array of computers employed by the network helps keep it reliable even during disruptions such as fires or power failures. Emergency phone calls generally swamp the system during those times. The network's computers then go into action, selecting and routing calls automatically through circuits that are not overtaxed.

In some cases an alternate route may take a call more than a thousand miles away from the originating point before it is completed. This can be accomplished so swiftly that a person making the call is unaware of how far the signal had to travel before completion.

The work of improving the nation's telecommunications network is never ending. One of the very latest developments is the use of light waves for transmission purposes. Although the method is new in that the technology has only now been brought to the practical stage, its potential usefulness was shown by Alexander Graham Bell more than one hundred years ago while he was working to perfect his telephone.

Sometimes referred to as photonics technology or optical or light wave communications, this system makes use of photons—elementary particles of light—instead of electrons to carry impulses. The photons travel through hair-thin glass fibers rather than through copper wire. The light sources for the photons may be laser beams or light-emitting diode devices. These and other electronic elements are integrated on a magic chip.

During operation the original electrical signal is converted into a light signal. En route to its destination, the light signal is kept up to normal strength by a series of boosters stationed along the transmission system. At the end of its journey, the light signal is changed back to an electrical signal.

The light wave transmission system has extraordinary advantages over more conventional methods. Fantastic signal speed and greater signal capacity are two of its more important superior features. A single glass fiber, thin as a human hair, can carry hundreds of times more bits of information per second than a conventional copper wire can handle. In the business world this superior performance of light wave communications for voice, data, and video translates into greater economy over the standard system in use.

The first full-service light wave system carrying voice, data, and video signals was constructed in Chicago in 1977.

The glass fiber "cables" proved highly successful

and are now being incorporated into the telecommunications network throughout the country.

Space science and technology at this writing are twenty-five years old. During this quarter of a century a number of exciting space events have taken place, including the launching into orbit of unmanned satellites designed to perform a variety of jobs. Among the first of these were telecommunications satellites.

The first space vehicle of this type was the primitive, balloonlike *Echo* satellite of 1960. Without electronic equipment of any sort, the *Echo* simply served as a reflector. Radio signals from an earth station bounced off the satellite and were relayed back to another receiving station on earth. The *Echo* was really a demonstration vehicle that helped to convince the scientists and engineers working with this communications concept that they were on the right track.

In 1962 the first electronic space relay station, *Telstar,* was sent into orbit. Electronic equipment aboard the spacecraft received signals flashed from earth stations, the signals were amplified aboard the satellite and then transmitted to another earthbound station.

This pioneering communications system immediately showed bright promise as an aid for upgrading communications not only within a single nation but also between nations. Today, that promise has been fulfilled with a fleet of such relay stations orbiting 22,400 miles above the earth.

Equipped with the most advanced microelectronics technology for transmission purposes, these

This is the Mission Control Center for the space shuttle flights. The banks of computers and telecommunications equipment provide the vital link with orbiting astronauts.

Courtesy Ford Aerospace and Communications Corporation

space relay stations are blanketing the globe with voice video, and data signals. Space transmission stations that aim their signals to a restricted area on earth are generally referred to as domestic satellites. Their signals are picked up by receiving stations within the borders of a single nation.

Domestic communications satellites are proving important in the development of pay television systems in the United States. Subscribers to the system install small dish-shaped antennas on the rooftops of their homes. These gather in the signals from space.

Among the advantages of this form of transmission are the increased number of channels the user can choose from. And, since the signals are direct and strong, reception is clearer.

Space relay transmissions can also send voice and data signals. The ability to transmit data enables large corporations to establish their own private communications network. The U.S. government also uses this means of communication to connect all of its embassies and military bases throughout the world.

We have mentioned only the highlights of today's telecommunications network in the United States. Many more elements make the network the largest, most complex such system in the world. Keeping this highly automatic, flexible, and intelligent communications network performing at top efficiency day in and day out is a truly Herculean task. It could not be done without the impressive support systems built into the network.

To carry out their specialized tasks, more than a hundred of these support systems make use of over four thousand minicomputers and three hundred maxicomputers. Without the assistance of these machines and their magic chips, our vast system of telecommunications could not operate.

Education

One of the more interesting applications of microelectronics—principally computers—is in the field of education. The computer has invaded the classroom and is fast becoming the most popular teacher in America's schools, from elementary to college level.

Among the earliest electronic teaching aids is a midget computer called Speak and Spell, made by Texas Instruments. It was designed for students from seven to twelve years of age. Over two hundred basic words, such as "ocean," "language," and "obey," are stored in the unit's memory chip. About the size of an average textbook, the machine contains a voice synthesizer that pronounces a word. The students then spell the word on the computer's screen. The computer praises students who spell the words correctly and tells them to try a second time if they misspell a word.

Today, electronic teaching tools have become a good deal more sophisticated than Speak and Spell, and thousands are in use at all school levels. They run the gamut of subjects taught from the three R's to advanced mathematics, science, and foreign languages. Some colleges, particularly those that offer technical courses, require their students to own computers.

A young student working a computer learning aid, System80, developed by the Borg-Warner Company.

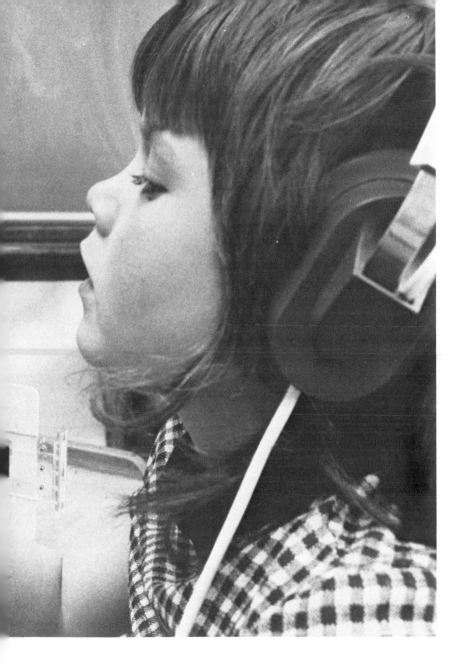

Many teachers are enthusiastic supporters of computers as teaching tools. They feel that students who work with these electronic machines pick up math skills faster and show a marked improvement in their ability to think logically and to organize subject matter. Language teachers have found the computer extremely useful for teaching foreign languages, an area where graduates of this country's schools appear to be deficient.

There is no denying that computers in the school classroom have generated vast interest and enthusiasm on the part of students. However, among educators these electronic teaching aids have not been unanimously accepted. Some teachers feel that the more traditional methods have greater value because they force students to rely on their own abilities rather than on a machine.

The computer itself has become a subject that students learn about in school. By acquiring the knowledge and skill to operate, program, or service computers students can prepare themselves for excellent jobs in a high-technology industry and can also become better equipped to cope with this increasingly computerized world.

Transportation

The success of one technical field very often depends on the technological advances made in another field. This is true of present-day commercial airline operations, which have developed as a result of advances in microelectronics. The airlines, in other words, could not carry on as they do without help from microelectronic equipment. High-speed, long-range jet flights, for example, would be hazardous undertakings without electronic flight and navigation instruments, computer-aided automatic pilots, radar, and telecommunications systems.

The help that microelectronics gives to airline operations comes in many other forms, too. At busy airports that handle hundreds of incoming and outgoing flights, air traffic controllers use radar, computers, and voice communications with pilots to prevent congestion and potential collisions.

Fog and low-hanging clouds over airports are threats to airplane pilots trying to bring their giant planes and human cargo safely to earth. Electronics has long been of help to them in doing the job efficiently and safely. Electronic equipment especially designed for the job provides an invisible glide path, which pilots pick up with their onboard instruments. This unseen electronic pathway in the sky enables the plane's flight crew to line up the aircraft with an obscured runway and land safely.

This instrument landing system is about to be upgraded with advanced microwave and computer equipment that will allow a greater number of planes to land within a given period more quickly and safely. Much of the landing operation up to the moment of touchdown will be taken care of by the new microelectronics system.

Pilots are required to fly their aircraft along invisible skyways that girdle the earth. They must stay at a certain altitude and follow a precise course when traveling in one direction. When traveling in the opposite direction they are required to fly at a differ-

This air traffic controller is entering into a computer information from a plan view display of airport incoming and outgoing flights.

ent altitude and on a different course. To help flight crews accomplish this, computers are now used to supplement the standard navigational instruments. Several electronic brains are generally installed aboard commercial airliners. The extra computers serve as backup units to support the original machine in case technical difficulties arise.

Before an airplane takes off, the crew members feed into the computer the necessary information about the route they are to fly: altitude, speed, and latitude and longitude over key checkpoints along the way. As the flight progresses, the computer screen will tell the pilot when the craft is flying over a checkpoint. If there is any deviation from these coordinates, the pilot will know that the plane is not on course. Computers have made navigation almost a routine matter.

The union between space technology and microelectronics was a natural development. Space travel needed the miniaturization and wizardry of microelectronics to launch the many historic flights that have taken place in the last twenty-five years. At the same time the requirements of space technology served as one of the more important stimulants in the development of microelectronic devices and equipment.

Given instructions before blast-off time, computers control and guide manned and unmanned space vehicles from the start to the end of their journeys. Computers were crucial to the astronauts' memorable landing on the moon, the unmanned flights to the very edge of the solar system, and the practical operation of the numerous working satellites spinning around our planet.

We are approaching a time when human beings will establish permanent factories, research laboratories, and even living quarters in outer space. Computers and their microchips will play a major role in the success of these developments.

Freight railroading is another complex activity that has benefited from the development of microelectronics. One of the railroad workers' major problems is keeping track of freight cars. This was an extremely difficult task before computers came into use. Now, however, microelectronics equipment, notably the computer, has made the task immeasurably easier. Today a computer system called Train II traces rolling stock and sends freight cars where they are needed accurately and speedily. The system covers the entire United States and parts of Canada and Mexico as well.

Passenger-carrying rail lines also make full use of computers and other electronic aids for safe, efficient service. The tasks these machines perform range from reservation and ticket sales to signal systems and maintenance.

Automobiles are another form of transportation improved by microelectronics. This development, at least with cars in the United States, began when gasoline became scarce and expensive as a result of the Arab oil boycott. Thereafter fuel conservation became a chief concern of drivers.

One way that auto manufacturers sought to help drivers achieve greater fuel economy was to devise a tiny computer control that precisely feeds gasoline to the engine. It enables cars to go farther on less fuel.

This success encouraged engineers to employ electronics for other car features. Their goal was to produce cars that were not only safer but also more comfortable and efficient. Thus, computer-based systems are now available that tell drivers by voice instructions that the oil pressure is low, that the key has been left in the ignition, or that headlights have been left on.

This system operates by means of a series of sensors located at strategic points in the car. When a sensor detects that a part of the car is not operating properly or should not be operating at all, it sends a signal to a computer, which passes the information along to the driver. One such device issues its instructions in three languages: English, Spanish, and French.

Microelectronics in the Home

For more than three decades the television set has been the most common piece of microelectronic equipment in the home. Now it has a rival—the computer, which is rapidly catching up in popularity. In fact, when the television set, the computer, and the telephone are interconnected, they can transform the American home into an entertainment, information, and work center.

The TV set's primary function—receiving programs flashed through the air—has been greatly expanded with video cassette recorders (VCRs) and players. Viewers who are unable to watch a favorite TV program can set the recorder to pick up the program automatically. The viewers can watch the recorded program whenever they have time.

Viewers can also buy cassettes of popular TV shows, sports events, and motion pictures and watch them with the aid of a VCR. Video games are also programmed on tape cassettes and can be played through a computer hooked up to the TV set.

The television set, personal computer, and telephone have also been linked together to form a home banking system. A client of a bank that is part of such a system can perform a number of banking tasks without leaving home: obtaining up-to-the-minute information on checking account balances, for example, paying bills, or transferring money from one account to another.

This banking service involves interconnected computerized terminals in the bank and in the customers' homes. The arrangement brings to mind a matter of growing concern to those who use such systems—security. All too frequently computer systems previously thought secure have been broken into by people who have no right to the information stored or transmitted by the computer service. One of the more serious break-ins of this sort occurred when a group of young computer whizzes in Milwaukee gained access to a computer system operated by a government laboratory engaged in secret nuclear weapons research.

The information they obtained was not important, but the break-in nevertheless alarmed officials in the Pentagon who are responsible for the nation's nuclear military secrets. This break-in and numerous others like it also aroused deep concern in the civilian sector where such computer systems are employed. No one involved with computer systems can say with certainty just how safe private matters are when they are entrusted to electronic equipment.

Computer and other electronics experts are burning the midnight oil in an effort to think of ways to prevent break-ins of computer systems. Two likely measures being worked on include unbreakable code systems and devices that scramble and unscramble information moving through a computer system.

Coming back to our discussion of electronics in the home, other types of computer systems are emerging that will permit individuals at home to shop at supermarkets, check on the availability of travel reservations, or find out the latest stock market quotations.

As an information center the home computer can make available almost 1,500 data sources or information banks scattered throughout the country. These provide facts on subjects ranging from gardening and cooking instructions to highly complex scientific data.

Computers and related electronic equipment can perform still other services within the home. They can automatically activate home security systems, house lights, and heating and air-conditioning equipment, thus acting as servants and guards.

Most of the home electronic conveniences mentioned here are only in their beginning stages. They promise to enrich our lives and make us a good deal more comfortable. But we are told that more surprises are in store as lively minds find new ways of putting the magic chip to work.

5

The Chip— Microelectronics— and the Future

For the past quarter-century we have witnessed an outpouring of amazing microelectronic devices—home computers, supercomputers, and cordless telephones, to mention but a few. They are altering our way of life as have few other modern technological creations.

In view of the bewildering array of microelectronic magic we are encountering, it is difficult to imagine what other wonders can be in store for us. Yet, if the predictions of the scientists and engineers working on the frontier of microelectronic technology are borne out, we are in for still greater and more startling developments in the future. The overall feeling of the experts is that we are actually on the threshold of a truly dazzling world of microelectronics that will come to pass in the years ahead.

The basis for these as yet unborn microelectronic wonders will be the microchip, just as this tiny device is responsible for the marvels of today. The major goal of research workers in the semiconductor field is to find ways of cramming many more kilobits of information on the fingernail-size chip.

A question may well come to mind at this point: Why the intense effort to crowd more data on a tiny chip that is already jammed with information? The reason is that the more data bits there are on a chip the closer its electronic circuits or switches will be to one another and therefore the faster the on-off pulses of electric current will move among the various circuits. Equipped with the superchips of tomorrow, computers will be capable of carrying out billions of calculating steps a second instead of the millions they are capable of handling today. Researchers are making progress toward their goal; right now a 500,000-plus chip is about to go into production. Before too many more years have passed, semiconductor manufacturers are confident that they will be making chips with one million or even three and four million kilobits.

Two problems that researchers will have to face and overcome concern overheating and cost. The densely packed circuits of an individual chip collectively could produce enough heat to interfere with the chip's efficient operation. Some form of cooling system almost surely will have to be devised.

Then too, cramming a chip with thousands of circuits will have to be done in such a way that the cost of manufacturing the device will not become prohibitive.

The avenues of research being explored in the hope they will lead to the chips of the future are numerous and unusual to say the least. Some laboratory workers are concentrating on advancing conventional chip technology by improving the basic semiconductor material itself. Instead of the universally used silicon, they are experimenting with less familiar materials such as gallium arsenide and the rare metal niobium.

Gallium offers considerable promise as a replacement for silicon. Laboratory success with the semiconductor material is leading researchers to believe that it will be on the market in a few years. Its electronic switching superiority is said to be about four times faster than silicon.

Because it is a rare material—far less common than silicon—gallium is a good deal more expensive, and this could restrict its use.

Other researchers are investigating supercold concepts and photon light particles. In certain tests, for example, scientists have piped helium into chambers to produce supercold conditions of minus 450 degrees Fahrenheit. They then immersed silicon chips, whose surfaces are crowded with microscopic off-on switches and other electronic elements, in this frigid bath. The supercold removed all resistance to the movement of electrons within the semiconductor material, thus permitting them to travel faster.

Should photons eventually prove to be effective operators of on-off switches in microchips, they will have brought an entirely different device into existence. Instead of electrons speeding through silicon chip circuits, photons will do the job. As we have already seen, their speed is superfast, since they move at the velocity of light—186,000 miles per second.

To accommodate the swiftness of photons, a new type of transistor called a transphoton had to be created. A solid-state device, it operates a thousand times faster than the conventional transistor.

As we have seen, photons are already being employed in light wave technology for telephone data and other forms of communications. With the proper miniaturization of components for the micro world of the chip, photons stand a good chance of becoming key workers in microelectronics of tomorrow.

Another approach that some researchers believe holds great promise is the use of a laser beam to etch complex circuit patterns on a silicon wafer. The intense light beam creates microscopic spots of superhot temperature on the wafer. The process is carried out inside a gas chamber. As the gas comes in contact with the spots, it alters the electrical characteristics of the silicon, causing some spots to become nonelectrical and others to become electrical. They become the transistors and other necessary electrical components that allow the chip to perform its work.

A computer guides the laser beam through the

circuit pattern that is to be etched. Extremely fast and powerful chips are expected to result from the use of the laser beam technique. In turn, the chips will advance the design and construction of computers, particularly the supercomputer types.

While many microchip research workers are searching for new ways to make silicon circuits faster and more powerful, others are working on completely different approaches that they hope will lead to the same results. Instead of concentrating on single silicon circuits, or microprocessers, they are experimenting with groups of circuits wired together that simultaneously tackle different portions of a computer problem.

Existing microchips enable computers to solve one calculating step at a time—division, subtraction, and the like. The new parallelism technique, as the group-circuit arrangement is called, would allow the computer to perform literally thousands of such steps at the same time. It would be used primarily in supercomputers.

One project involving the development of parallelism is leading to a supercomputer that its builders expect will far outstrip any such machine now operating. This number-cruncher will be a math whiz of dazzling proportions, capable of making six billion additions a second. It will be able to do this because of the parallel hookup of its thousands of tiny microprocessor circuits, each of which can move at an amazing speed.

This unusual computer has yet to go into full-scale operation. Wiring its components is an enormously complex task, and many things can go wrong, but its makers are confident of success. When this computer goes into operation, it is expected to be the progenitor of a whole new breed of awesome supercomputers.

Supercomputers will be the main beneficiaries of the research producing more powerful and faster microchips. (Any machine capable of performing more than twenty million operations a second is considered a supercomputer.) These enormously complex and costly machines are considered the top performers of computer technology, and well they might be. There are about six of them in existence—all made in the United States—that can whiz through calculating steps at the rate of 100 million per second. Some can accomplish 400 million for short bursts. The next generation of these number-crunchers will far outperform their predecessors by doing multiplication and addition at a speed of more than a billion calculations a second.

Supercomputers are not for home or even business use, however. They carry a price tag of over ten million dollars, for one thing, and are so complex that they require professional operation. Furthermore, the supercomputers' capabilities greatly exceed the needs of the individual computer user.

Supercomputers are useful when enormously long and involved calculations are required. A single problem may call for as many as ten trillion calculations. One area in which they are used is nuclear physics research. As a matter of fact, for this type of work supercomputers are considered the most valuable tool to come along in decades. Scientists studying intercontinental ballistic missile trajectories also find the supercomputer enormously valuable. Cracking secret codes of unfriendly nations—cryptology—and formulating other codes to protect domestic military and government secrets is another area in which supercomputers are put to work. Meteorologists who study and forecast the weather are finding the supercomputer an enormous boon for their difficult task, too.

As we all are pretty much aware, the weather is difficult to predict. It is constantly changing, and weather experts are hard put to keep up with the continuously changing factors on which they base their forecasts. Supercomputers handle meteorological data with ease.

British forecasters, for example, are finding a supercomputer helpful for keeping up with the highly variable weather of their country. They feed something like fifty million items of weather data into their calculating whiz. The machine digests this input with 800 million calculations. The output data enable the forecasters to make a five-day weather forecast every fifteen minutes. The newer number whizzes will devour even more data and will help forecasters predict the weather more accurately and sooner.

Aircraft designers studying the flow of air over projected new designs, geologists analyzing data on the earth's substrata while searching for petroleum, and even the people who make motion pictures all use supercomputers to speed up and enhance their work. The motion picture *Tron* was the first to make large-scale use of supercomputers to create unusual visual effects. The technique excited great interest, and other films will use the new supercomputers for more stunning imagery.

As noted earlier, all the supercomputers in operation today carry a made-in-America label. Two companies have had a monopoly on their manufacture—Cray Research, Inc., and Control Data Corporation. The Cray I, first of the commercial supercomputers, is a leader of its kind. The computer by Control Data, the CYBER 205, is second. Both machines, using thousands of 64 K memory and logic chips, can perform operations in the 100-million-per-second range.

These two supercomputer companies are building newer models that will work at twice the speed of their predecessors. A newly developed and far more powerful 250 K chip will provide these new giants with their lightning-swift capabilities.

But even these supercomputers are destined to reign over the computer world only a short time, because semiconductor researchers are promising newer and more powerful chips in the near future. In the summer of 1983 IBM announced that it had developed a successful new microchip having more than twice the power of the 250 K model. Equipped with these new performers, supercomputers capable of 400 million operations per second won't be long in coming. And the work of developing this new generation of supercomputers is no longer limited to Cray Research and Control Data.

Government-supported laboratories and research agencies, university research centers, and a newly established consortium of a dozen private semiconductor and computer companies have formed a private research group, the Microelectronics and Computer Technology Corporation. The group is closely involved with efforts to build the most powerful supercomputers possible.

Nor is current supercomputer development confined solely to the United States. Japanese scientists and engineers are also engaged in a major effort. Indeed, just as the Japanese successfully challenged the U.S. computer industry in other areas of technology, so too are they determined to become leaders in the manufacture of supercomputers.

The commercial stakes on a worldwide basis are high, and to help them achieve their goal, the Japanese have established a research program with $200 million provided by the government. Before the decade of the 1980s ends, they hope to create a supercomputer a thousand times faster than the Cray I.

The business of building more powerful and faster supercomputers is rapidly becoming a spirited international competition. This country wishes to maintain its leadership; the Japanese are eager to take it away. At this point the United States has the advantage mainly because of its long lead in developing and building supercomputers. But American scientists are fully aware of the high caliber of Japan's technological achievements, and no one in the computer field in the United States is taking their competition lightly.

The U.S. Defense Department is particularly concerned about Japan's progress in developing supercomputers. In light of the vital role the supercomputer plays in this country's defenses, military planners do not want the source of the best supercomputer to be a foreign country. In an effort to prevent this from happening, the military is supporting supercomputer research and development work through its Advanced Research Projects Agency.

Right now it appears that the supercomputers of tomorrow will be involved strictly with numbers; they will be lightning-swift calculators, in other words. However, scientists and engineers are striving to bring into existence a second type with greater "brain" power. These intelligent machines will have the ability to "think" and "reason." Their operators will be able to speak or write to them, and the machines will carry out instructions. These "brainy" computers will also be able to recognize objects.

The future supercomputers would be superfast with numerical calculations up to a point. Thereafter their "brain" power would function by interpreting symbols instead of numbers.

Because these superintelligent computers have enormous potential for the development of futuristic war equipment—pilotless aircraft, for example, and unmanned submarines—this country's military technical experts vigorously support their development.

Japanese scientists and engineers, determined not to be left behind, are involved in research that seeks to create this same type of superintelligent computer.

The technical fallout from all the research aimed at building more powerful supercomputers will surely benefit the development of personal, business, and industrial computers. These far more common machines will have larger, better memories; they will be faster performers; and they will become a good deal more versatile. The versatility of industrial computers will be particularly evident in the improvement of automation and robots.

In 1983 there were 15,000 robots at work in U.S. factories, most of them doing welding and painting chores in automobile and aircraft plants.

By the end of this century the number of robots in use is expected to increase to nearly 300,000. Equipped with "seeing" and "feeling" devices, they will be far more intelligent than the present generation of robots, and their tasks will include more complicated activities. For example, they will be able to select a nut, bolt, or other small component and attach it properly to the product being assembled.

Such highly sophisticated robots may one day cause a good deal of distress by taking over the jobs of human workers. Robots may equal or even outnumber human laborers in some factories by the end of the century.

Robots of tomorrow will work not only in industrial plants on earth but also in space factories. According to space experts, such factories will orbit the earth at 200- or 300-mile altitudes by the year 2000. Pharmaceutical products of the utmost purity; ball bearings that, in the gravity-free environment of space, would be far superior to those made in earthbound factories; and microelectronic components, especially semiconductors, whose manufacture demands surroundings of extreme cleanliness, seem likely to be the earliest products to be manufactured in space.

The TeachMover is a tabletop robot arm whose movements are controlled by a microprocessor chip in its base. A hand-held control box is used for its operation. As its name tells us, the robot is mainly a tool for teaching—in this case, the fundamentals of robotics. Engineers involved with production processes also find it helpful for designing and refining industrial robot stations.

Courtesy Microbot, Inc.

No human workers will run the first space factories. Instead, the work will be performed by a hybrid of the earthbound robots, a teleoperated type. This robot has no programmed independent intelligence like earthbound robots, but instead is instructed in what to do by a human operator at a distant location. These robots were created in the early 1950s, mainly to handle hazardous materials at nuclear research centers.

Electronics workers in the space factory will probably be controlled from earth stations or from spacecraft flying some distance from the factories. Instructions will be sent to the space automatons by radio. Equipped with electromechanical arms, grabbers (hands), and sensory components, the automatons will respond by doing the required production operations.

Packaging the finished products and loading them on space shuttle freighters will also be carried out by radio-controlled robots. Later, these robots may well be joined in the factories by human workers who will supervise and monitor them.

The electronic space automatons are also expected to play a vital role in the construction of space factories. Moving about in space by means of their small power thrusters, teleoperated robots will position the lightweight prefabricated parts of a factory in space and fasten them together. Their operators will observe and control the robots from a nearby orbiting space shuttle.

All this may sound like science fiction, but a good many of these futuristic developments have already taken place. Nearly all of the spectacular achievements in space over the past twenty-five years have been accomplished by teleoperated robots. The one major exception was the moon landing in 1969.

The most fantastic space feat carried out by the teleoperator robot took place in 1976. After a space journey of three hundred days *Viking One* and *Viking Two* arrived in the vicinity of Mars. Telecommunicated instructions from earth activated the spacecrafts' highly sophisticated computer-controlled guidance and landing systems. Both space vehicles, on different days, descended through the Martian atmosphere to that planet's strange, red-colored surface.

After landing, the electromechanical arms and scoops (hands) aboard the spacecraft were instructed to dig into the red soil. Onboard cameras took pictures of the historic event, which were flashed back to earth nearly 50 million miles away via telecommunications.

A more recent demonstration of a teleoperated robot working successfully in space occurred in 1983. When the space shuttle *Challenger* made its journey into the cosmos, it carried in its cargo bay a Canadian-built scientific research satellite. After *Challenger* reached the desired orbit, the electromechanical arm aboard the shuttle—called a *R*emote *M*anipulator *S*ystem (RMS)—lifted the satellite out of the bay and deposited it on station. Sally Ride, the first American woman to orbit in space, operated the robotic arm.

In the future, by using such a teleoperated robotic

arm, astronauts aboard a space shuttle will be able to repair satellites that are no longer operating. If necessary, the robotic arm will lift them into the shuttle's bay for return to earth and will put a new satellite on the station.

By the end of this decade, we may actually be using robots in our homes. They will serve as electronic servants, bringing us the newspaper or a cup of tea and opening the door for visitors. Other household robots will vacuum and dust our rooms. The really smart ones may even cook our meals. A robotic creature of this sort already exists in the form of an office mail deliverer. This electronic automaton makes its rounds on a specific route within an office and between offices.

Along with robots, our homes may someday be equipped with an array of sophisticated microelectronic equipment. In more than 80 percent of all homes minicomputers will control the heating, air conditioning, and security and will help students with their homework.

Home computers will also make it possible to link up with scores of different computer systems— medical data banks, library information sources, travel and reservation facilities, electronic mail services, banks, and numerous other commercial services. Many of these electronic conveniences are already here, as we have seen.

The home video-computer center will be very versatile. As an entertainment facility it will offer direct TV transmission from orbiting satellites. This will benefit regions that now have poor reception or a

An experimental home information system developed by Bell Laboratories. Keyboard terminals of the system are hooked up to modified color TV sets. The system allows users to obtain news, pay bills, shop, or buy transportation tickets.

limited selection of channels. Many more programs will be available.

Serious governmental matters will also be affected by home computers. In a democracy such as ours many citizens do not exercise their right to vote. This is all too painfully evident during presidential elections. Political and civic groups have again and again made vigorous efforts to get voters to the polls, but they have never been very successful. Now, through the use of microelectronics, this state of affairs may change.

A special telecommunications hookup will enable people to vote in local, state, and national elections without ever leaving their homes. This electronic innovation may also be used to take the census. It would be less costly and faster than the cumbersome door-to-door system now used.

As for home appliances and other electronic gadgets, the list of possibilities for the future is almost endless. To cite a few examples: cordless telephones are available and growing in popularity; conventional telephones can now store important numbers, make calls, and record messages automatically. Other devices are being worked on that will be even more computerlike in their capabilities by the time this century comes to an end. Someday, for instance, the kitchen stove will be able to prepare food automatically at a preset time so that when a person returns home, the evening meal will be ready to eat.

Those who like to predict future happenings are having a field day describing warfare in the twenty-first century. The changes that futurists see will radically alter centuries-old methods of fighting on land

Supermarket customers may soon be using a special debit card to pay for groceries through an electronic system.

and sea and in the air. War is expected to enter the world of space employing weapons of fantastic performance and destructive ability.

The popular motion picture *Star Wars* graphically depicted a war of the future. The fictional weapons in that picture made those in use today look like toys. If ever space weapons of the *Star Wars* type come into existence, one can be certain their incredible abilities will be due in large measure to the microchip.

As of this moment a realistic concept of what defense weapons of the future might be like would include incredibly fast supercomputers, laser beams, or destructive particle rays that are still being researched in laboratories. Combined with spacecraft of exotic forms and performance, the weapons would be used to ward off attacking intercontinental nuclear missiles.

Sensitive, fast-acting microelectronic detection equipment installed on space platforms would spot the incoming missiles, radar would track them, and laser beams or other rays would destroy them before they could reach their targets. Such weapons systems now exist only in the minds of military scientists, however. Developing them will be quite a different story. Many scientists do not believe that such weapons should ever be built. But President Ronald Reagan and many other people think that the weapons of tomorrow can and must be created. President Reagan strongly supports the start of a U.S. research and development program leading toward that goal.

Conventional weapons of war are also expected to be radically transformed by microelectronics. The combined use of satellites, cameras, computers, and telecommunications systems will make entire battle zones visible to generals and their staffs at headquarters. The more conventional means of learning what is going on in the battle zone is by way of field telephones and colored pins stuck in huge maps.

With the use of tomorrow's electronic pictorial battle system, defenders of an area could make swift countermoves to fend off an attack. Indeed, battle movements are expected to be so swift and fluid that only with the help of computers would generals have sufficient and correct data to decide on the proper countermoves.

By employing computers, radar, and the like, battle commanders could deceive an opposing general into believing that an imaginary army was massing at a critical point. Rushing forces to defend the area, the general would be unable to fight off the real attack at another point. The opponent's surveillance system would be thoroughly deceived by the illusory computerized radar signals. This scheme is expected to be effective for naval operations, too, by depicting phantom fleets on an enemy's radar screens.

As for the actual hardware or battlefield weapons, artillery shells and land-based missiles are going to be a lot smarter and far more destructive than those now employed. Much of their effectiveness will be due to the microchip. Equipped with miniature sensing devices, cruise missiles will find and home in on enemy targets hundreds of miles distant through all kinds of weather. The missiles will have a special computer brain that will permit them to take evasive action if they are attacked by aircraft or other missiles.

Communication systems are crucial in wartime. Battles have been won and lost because one side or the other had superior or inadequate information about what was taking place on the battlefield. Laser beams are expected to be an important means of improving military communications in tomorrow's warfare. As we know from their civilian applications at the moment, these light rays are capable of handling enormous quantities of data in seconds.

It is a sad fact that microelectronics, often said to be the most significant technical development since the creation of the steam engine, is feverishly being adapted by the people of one nation to destroy the inhabitants of other countries. Perhaps, when the destructive powers of these weapons are truly realized, people will pause and think about what they are doing. We can hope that they will then decide to junk all such destructive projects.

If by some miracle this should come to pass, then the tiny microchip, essential to the effectiveness of such weapons, will indeed be rightly described as the magic chip.

Glossary

Automation—A manufacturing or industrial process performed automatically by a device or equipment that is mechanical, electromechanical, or electronic in nature.

BASIC—One of the earliest languages developed for operating a computer. The relatively simple and now standard code was created by John Kemeny and Thomas Kurtz, two pioneer computer scientists. The word derives from *B*eginners *A*ll-purpose *S*ymbolic *I*nstruction *C*ode.

Binary—An arithmetical code system consisting of two digits, 0 and 1.

Bit—*Bi*nary digi*t*, the 1 or the 0 in the binary arithmetical system, the smallest unit in a computer's data bank.

Byte—An informational unit formed by a group of bits representing letters or numbers; eight bits constitute a byte.

Cathode Ray Tube (CRT)—An electronic tube similar to the picture tube in a television receiver; a controlled beam of electrons sprayed on the fluorescent inner surface of the tube is transformed into numbers, letters, or graphics.

Central Processing Unit (CPU)—A chip that can function as the basic memory or logic center of a computer. Also referred to as a microprocessor and often called the "brain" of the computer; it controls processing and execution of programmed instructions.

151

Chip—A tiny sliver of semiconductor material containing electronic components of an integrated circuit designed to perform a specific function. Most computers have more than one chip. Fixed to slim plastic boards, chips are interconnected by hair-thin wire.

Circuit—A specific track or avenue having all the needed components for the controlled movement of electrons.

Computer—An electronic machine capable of receiving coded data and processing it in accordance with another set of instructions into a form for some practical use.

Disc drive—The unit that spins the discs in a computer and receives information from or gives it to the disc. In computer language this is called "reading" and "writing."

Floppy disc—A thin, flexible plastic disc similar to a phonograph record, containing the data that computers process and the instructions or software programs that tell computers what to do.

Integrated circuit—An extremely compact group of electronic elements—transistors, capacitors, and so forth—interconnected to form a working circuit. Reduced to microscopic proportions, the circuitry is implanted on a sliver (chip) of silicon called a substrate.

Microcomputer—A desktop computer for general purpose use. It is faster and more versatile than the smaller minicomputer.

Microsecond—One-millionth of a second.

Modem—*Mo*dulator and *dem*odulator, a device that changes electronic signals from a computer into sounds for telephone transmission. At the receiving end, the modem reconverts the sounds back into electronic signals.

Module—A separate electronic unit that can easily be interconnected with another electronic unit, like a computer.

Nanosecond—One-billionth of a second.

Program—A set of instructions telling a computer exactly how to function.

Programmer—A person who writes computer instructions.

Robot—An automatic machine or device that can perform functions equivalent to those carried out by human beings.

Semiconductor—A material with electrical properties that can be altered to increase or restrict the flow of electrons.

Solid-state device—A device made from a solid semiconductor material and capable of electronic activity. Unlike the vacuum tube, which it has largely displaced, the solid-state does not require a vacuum.

Word processor—A desktop computer that enables an operator to write, edit, and print text material.

Further Reading

BOOKS

Barcomb, David. *Office Automation: A Survey of Tools and Techniques.* Bedford, Massachusetts: Digital Press, 1981.

Evans, Christopher. *The Making of the Micro —A History of the Computer.* New York: Van Nostrand Reinhold, 1981.

Forester, Tom, ed. *The Microelectronic Revolution.* Cambridge, Massachusetts: MIT Press, 1981.

Krasnoff, Barbara. *Robots: Reel To Real.* New York: Arco Publishing, 1982.

Lecht, Charles P. *The Waves of Change.* New York: McGraw-Hill, 1979.

McWilliams, Peter A. *The Word Processing Book.* Los Angeles, California: Prelude Press, 1982.

This list is a sampling of the vast literature concerning the microchip and microelectronics in general. The Subject Guide to Books in Print lists many more titles in areas of particular interest.

PERIODICALS

For the latest development in microelectronics, periodicals are indispensable sources. The following are some articles of interest.

"Computers: A New Wave," *Newsweek,* February 23, 1976.

Index

"How the Car Computer Is Changing Detroit," *Business Week*, October 22, 1979.

"The Impudent Magical Silicon Chip," *Horizon*, July, 1977.

"The Micros Take to The Classroom," *Business Week*, July 23, 1979.

Readers will also find articles of interest in various issues of *Scientific American, Science, New Science, Hi-Tech, Science Digest,* and *Popular Science.*

Index

157

About the Author

A full-time writer for more than thirty years, Frank Ross, Jr., has over fifty books to his credit, including *The Metric System,* a Junior Literary Guild Selection; and *Space Shuttle,* named an Outstanding Science Book for Children in 1979 by the National Science Teachers Association.

The author has made the fields of science and technology his particular specialization.

Frank Ross and his wife Laura—also an author of children's books, and a former librarian—live in Southampton, Long Island, New York.